Law of Attraction

by Julia Meadows

About the Author

Julia Meadows is a senior life coach and Wellness expert at the WellnessMastership.com, a life coaching business based in London, England.

Wellness Mastership teaches clients on consciousness, lifting your vibration, the real law of attraction (updated), and the art of living a better life. Through our teaching we have helped clients worldwide gain a better advantage, and help develop themselves and achieve more from want they desire.

WANT A COPY OF MY NEW EBOOK?

Email me:
WellnessMastership@gmail.com

Table of Contents

Introduction

Life is never in a constant phase. It moves on and on. A time comes it changes the direction of our lives. We get thoughts on how we will pursue our life, but it's been proven that when we want something to happen it happens as we think it will. So it all depends upon our image of how we see things, unlike getting things to be done in just the way it is, but it is not possible without proper planning. Sadly, so many of us are actually incognizant about the strength and potential that is bolted inside us. As a result, we leave our contemplations and feelings unchecked. Such an action conveys some unacceptable musings and draws in more undesirable feelings and occasions into our life. Human thoughts should encompass an aim-oriented flow of ideas and associations that can lead to a reality-oriented conclusion. An important aspect of this philosophy is modifying one's negative thinking patterns into positive ones. Besides, one should also "feel" (through inventive visualization) that the required changes in the thinking pattern have already occurred. This mix of positive thought and positive feeling is believed to draw in positive experiences and opportunities. It is possible because of the resonance between positivity and planned energetic law. Therefore, if you stay focused on the good in your life, you will be attracted to the good and vice versa. If you focus on the shortcomings, then that will be the focus of your life. As an attraction, if you feel happy, passionate, loving, happy, appreciative, or overflowing, then you are sending positive energy. Through the Law of Attraction, the atmosphere will respond enthusiastically to both of these movements. It doesn't decide which one is best for you. It just responds to any energy you build, giving you the same. You get exactly what you put in there.

Whatever you think and feel at any given time has your application in the universe in the same vein. Because your vibration will attract energy to the same waves, you need to make sure that you continuously transmit the energy, thoughts, and feelings associated with what you want to be, doing, and experience. The energy level needs to match what you want to attract in your life. If happiness and love are what you want to attract, then the vibrating waves should be positive.

Many people have confusing beliefs that prevent them from allowing abundance and happiness in their lives. If this is you, be aware that you must first transform your limiting beliefs. into Thoughts that are appropriate, lovable, desirable, and competent and wise enough, powerful enough, attractive enough, rich enough, sufficient, and in every way essential to you. Once you believe you will get what you want, the second part of the math is to take action. Taking steps to create the results you want reaffirms your belief that you can achieve what you want.

Your attitude is proportional to what you overcome, or how high you can rise above the temptations and sorrows of the world, and to what extent you can conquer the feeling of selfishness. With a truly positive attitude and consistent religious beliefs, you will eventually find yourself in Paradise.

Besides, a negative attitude from a problem-solving mind will lead to compulsion and forced solutions, which will never lead to a positive or healthy outcome. When we look at life with a limited and constrained state of fear, doubt, and unbelief, it is not surprising that our lives become more complex, governed by adverse events and circumstances. When working from a negative perspective, it is not surprising that we sink quickly when we fight hard.

But, it is not a permanent storm. It requires that we not force the solutions but rather make internal changes. Thus controlling our external circumstances by first controlling our inner mental state. We create change first by adjusting our situation and paradigm. The Law of Attraction allows for endless possibilities, unlimited abundance, and endless happiness. They know the order of the difficulty, and it can change your life in every way.

Our life is full of great turns, and we will face many challenges that will teach us the lessons important to face the upcoming ones and to cope with the existing ones. However, we don't have anything else except our thought process, either negative or positive, which decides the outcomes. If we treat a challenge as a simple piece of work we can handle it easily, but if we complicate it, we are more likely to see the negativity. Such outcomes are due to our complicated and negative thought, and they will be devastating.

"The secret of success is to try always to improve yourself no matter where you are or what your position. Learn all you can. Don't see how little you can do, but how much you can do."

William Walker Atkinson Quote

We want things that we don't actually accept that we can have or can make occur. The energy of our considerations, how we feel about them, it's simply not line up with what we think we need. To show our commitment to what we want, we need to ensure our inner mind is prepared to center its energy similarly.

The Law of Attraction is consistently grinding a way in your life if you get it; if you trust it. It can work for you, and it can neutralize you; it can attempt to improve your life and permit you to be cheerful, or it can try to make life hard for you and cause you to be hopeless. The uplifting news about this reality is that you control what direction the Law of Attraction works in your day-to-day existence. The right direction can turn into motivation for some people. It can reveal individuals' actual possibilities and find the genuine legend that falsehoods have inserted in every last one of them. It can help achieve positive changes in individuals' lives concerning wellbeing, profession, and relationship. Life excursion is thrown with plenty of troublesome conditions and blustery happenings, where confidence shakes, contemplations become unclear, activities fixed, and dreams immaterialized. Individuals feel an absence of plenitude of well-being, riches, cash, achievement, and connections. They take a stab at force, strength, and internal satisfaction. Rhonda Byrne unfurls the key to the brain's imperceptible force that can change everyone's predetermination. The conviction or confidence that one can achieve the ideal objective can't arise except confidence in one's own capacity and force.

Therefore, Swami Vivekananda says:

"All power lies within you".

At the point when one builds up firm confidence in oneself that he would get what he had focused on, his energy gets lined up with the genuine source, a wellspring of boundless prospects since everything comes because of the vibration energy or recurrence that one ship off the universe, one must interface with it.

The Law of Attraction has been perceived for millennia; however, the individuals who comprehended its force didn't need everybody to approach finding out about it, so they kept it a mystery. At that point, the film and book by Rhonda Byrne, The Secret, burst upon the world, and a large number of normal societies began to investigate and comprehend the Law of Attraction. The law of attraction works through the force of gratitude. If one feels appreciative of what one now has, the law of attraction will pull in a greater amount of that and present it to one's life. Appreciation opens the best approach to the bounty of cash, wellbeing, riches, relationship, and material accomplishments. It helps in defeating the negative considerations and letting positive contemplations progression as a top priority.

The entire general climate will be filled with energy that transmits a recurrence that the sky is the limit that one longs for. One is a vigorous individual and has all the essentialness and vivacity to achieve anything. Such a demeanor or ability moves one with a limitless force. It will offer ascent to sentiments that one is forced to bear getting all the things and discover incredible harmony and comfort in accepting that one will get all that when it is lined up with the most elevated desires. This life on earth is an uncommon advantage. It is an honored blessing. For this, one owes appreciation to the All-powerful, who has given a delightful life to value, look about adoration, excellence, nature, contemplations, feelings, sentiments, the obvious and the imperceptible things of the universe. The term appreciation holds incredible importance. 'Appreciation' is a demonstration of gratefulness or the craft of passing on gratitude to somebody who has profited one in any way. It rises out of the core of one's being and, now and again, communicated through words, or signals, or activities. It is a mind-blowing center. It gives one a lifestyle.

At this point when you consider what you need, you are drawing in what you require to fulfill your need. This is the point when you are pondering what you don't need, you are drawing in what you would prefer not to have. The Universe will bring you what you ask for.

Chapter 1:
Money

Money isn't as simple as it seems. Numerous individuals trying to utilize the law of attraction expect to draw in a few types of abundance into their lives, amongst which money is prominent. By all means, an abundance of money is a critical aspect in numerous things we want to do, from enjoying a luxurious lifestyle complete with our fantasy houses to voyaging and ruining our friends and family with extravagant and liberal endowments. A lot of us have enormous, extravagant dreams that require finance to satisfy those fantasies. On the off chance that you, as well, have dreams that you wish to satisfy and require the assets for this purpose. At that point, you are likely inquisitive about how we all can utilize the law of attraction to pull in such abundance! This piece of the book will investigate how the law of attraction functions with riches and significant practices you can use to help you produce more noteworthy wealth in your life.

Concerning money, there are numerous ways that the law of attraction can help you assemble it. You can utilize the law of appreciation to help you pay your charges on schedule, to help you in finding or winning surprising cash, to increment your ordinary pay, to assist you with creating types of pay, and indeed, even to discover ways that you can leave on new changes that will result in you creating more pay. On the off chance that you are searching for a chance to increment your abundance in general, or in a particular way, the law of attraction can help you. Utilizing the law of attraction in assistance ensures the gathering of wealth and richness as a progressing practice, or it tends to be done in short blasts whereby you work to pull in explicit sums in aforementioned periods. For instance, if you need to buy a vehicle in the following three months, you may increase your expectations to pursue pulling in more cash that you can use to buy a vehicle within the following three months. Or then again, if you need to build your wealth for another reason or all in all constantly, you can utilize a standard abundance producing custom that will help you increment your riches.

How regularly you complete this training will determine your wanted outcomes and what monetary objectives you have for yourself. Generally advantageous results, nonetheless, suggest that you have some continuous wealth building work on going on This is similar to the condition where you utilize explicit practices for explicit conditions, for example, covering the tabs on schedule or paying for an excursion you want to take, or something else.

Cash is the establishment that permits security and openings in all everyday issues you care about the most. As far as I might be concerned, that is the motivation to often think about your offer, shoot by becoming your monetary base, and be pleased with the great heading you take.

You can utilize the Law of Appreciation to draw in anything you need, including cash. However, you may discover it is simpler to start by removing the simple thing you need rather than the money. This usually is because the majority of us have numerous mind hindrances that associate everything we want with cash and abundance. So, if you can work around the squares, you'll see, you can pull in what you need without essentially going through money.

Keep in mind, cash is essentially a mechanism of trade – an instrument or an asset we use to purchase the things and encounters we need. So frequently, we erroneously believe that it is cash itself we need. All things considered; we genuinely need the stuff we can do with money. For instance, you may think you need to draw in cash to take care of your Mastercard bills (I've been there!). In fact, what you truly need is an inclination of wealth, security, or opportunity. On the off chance that you had the Visa obligation and a lot of pay coming in to take care of those tabs, you'd be upbeat. There isn't sufficient cash that you think you need to pull in more money.

This is on the grounds that you are zeroing in on the absence of cash rather than the rich wealth in your life.

The arrangement isn't really to pull in more or show cash. All things being equal, you need to make the right relationship with cash. Your obligation is a blessing, and it can tell you the best way to make a special relationship with cash.

As far as I might be concerned, that is the motivation to often think about your total assets, shoot by extending your monetary base, and be pleased with the great course you take.

With one straightforward number, my absolute worth indicates my day-by-day obligation to those things that I care about the most. Our worth goes up because I settle on the day by day choices to ensure it remains as such. When it goes up, I realize that those aspects of my life that I care about are protected and solid, and can withstand startling occasions stunning decisions.

What amount is excessive? Its answer is basic. I realize that I am centered on amassing riches, and it isn't sufficient in different parts of my life when I see that balance and earnestly lament the things that have been left fixed. I don't have that feeling by any means - obviously, I can consider a couple of things I may have done another way, yet nothing truly fills me with laments. There isn't anything amiss with our monetary change at present when I take a gander at our monetary circumstance and think, "Well, I wish I might have done this other thing as opposed to building this security spine and the main chance."

There will be a time in my life when I feel that way, and that is where I need to ponder my monetary decisions going ahead. Are there things I can do with this monetary establishment that never occurred, things that permit me to live those needs and the key jobs I esteem truly?

Everything I can say is that it hasn't occurred to me strongly enough that I would regret it, and I don't even see it happening at any point shortly.

Eventually, everything boils down to one straightforward thought: the motivation behind your life isn't to bring in additional cash. The reason for your life is to discover who you need to be in this world and afterward utilize your cash to grow those jobs.

Like all the other things known to humanity, cash is energy. Cash is the apparent estimation of another energy that we trade it for, similar to a vehicle, shoes, food, and so forth. We trade cash for it to encounter and appreciate the energy of the vehicle, shoes, or food. We realize that all energy vibrates at its specific recurrence, so cash likewise has a vibration. You are additional energy, and your vibration either reverberates with that of cash or doesn't. How and what you feel about cash impacts your reverberation with it. If you have a positive outlook on cash, your reverberation is positive, and cash streams easily to you and through you. So, if you have any negative sentiments about cash, your vibration will obstruct cash progression, and you will end up inclination an absence of it.

I need to be known as an audience; an individual who helps and aides where important is to uplift the overall character and outlook. My monetary achievement encourages me to satisfy each of those parts, however only to a reasonable extent. When I settle on decisions that help my funds, I fortify every one of those activities. When I settle on poor monetary decisions, I peer down on every one of those activities.

The motivation behind your life isn't to be monetarily only. You must be good face-to-face, and monetary achievement is far off in advancing that sort of achievement.

One is qualified for esteem. It has worth, and you can't actually erase it. That is the thing that individuals need to comprehend.

For the most part, individuals believe that offering cash or worth is a hint of eagerness. We judge individuals by how they act to bring in cash. We are reluctant to state it for all to hear, for as much cash as individuals suspect. No spirit is apathetic regarding cash—we as a whole long for things. We, as a whole, satisfy our essential cravings by utilizing money. So we can't really isolate individuals or gap them.

I recall individuals uproariously saying that they realized that cash was nothing throughout everyday life. Note: it has its worth. The clothes we wear to cover our sleeves and the food we eat to keep us healthy, etc., state it is purchased with cash. Any individual who asserts that cash isn't significant in any way, to seem caring, is really loaded up proudly and requests consideration.

We need cash. How else would you be able to deal with pay for food? How might you discover somewhere else to live? If you see people in good clothing - recollect that they, as well, pay for convenience.

Anything you bring in has to do with cash.

There are numerous sorts of bliss. A few people can purchase those blessings, and that cash can't get it.

Do you truly need a pleasant, agreeable house to live in? It would help if you had cash. Want great food to appreciate with your companion? Cash. Going to travelling? Cash. But what's more that the cash won't bring back the dead or any individual who wishes to be missing from your life.

There are things you can purchase and things you can't accept. Your joy relies upon it.

What's more, guess what? There isn't anything amiss with needing cash. There isn't anything wrong with cash. Since cash is illicit, you buckle down, utilize your work and resourcefulness to get paid. You are exchanging for something, so the cash close by is yours. It's yours, totally.

Nonetheless, it closes when individuals go overboard to how they can manage cash. What's more, cash can crush an individual. Cash can fill an individual with voracity and conceal everything. That is the place where you battled against humanity. We need to confront reality and acknowledge it: Money is basic to life. All things considered, cash ought not to control us. It ought not to be underestimated. Cash has its worth. You leave it where it ought to be. Its significance, nonetheless; it's up to you.

Cash isn't simply the reason. Cash is the establishment that permits security and openings in all everyday issues you care about the most. In my opinion, this is the motivation to often think about your money as your only resort.

There are a couple of approaches to help you change your negative emotions about cash to begin pulling in a greater amount of it for you. These may appear to be strange to your convictions and perspective, yet they show you the amount you need to change what you accept to be valid about cash.

• Look at what you accept to be valid about cash and wealth.

Do these convictions reverberate with wellness according to you? Do you truly trust them to be valid, or could you accept something other than what's expected?

• Be thankful for what you have.

While you are centered around a sensation of need, you can't draw in cash. Be thankful for what you have now, as of now. Push away the sensations of requiring more since you don't have enough; simply be appreciative for what you have. Cause a rundown of the things you have that cash has empowered you to have and appreciate them. Every day, recall some of them as you state how thankful you are – in your considerations, for all to hear, and on paper – any way you feel good.

• Approach cash with deference.

Focus on your cash; notice how it streams into your life and where you spend it; learn about cash through an investigation into speculation, reserve funds plan, how to make circumstances to bring you more cash. Appreciate the cash that gets through your reality, acknowledges what it brings as far as you might be concerned, and takes great consideration of the cash that is in your ownership at any one time. Comprehend the estimation of cash and spend it carefully.

• Part with it.

You may be thinking, "What? I need more cash for my own requirements! I can't give any away!!" That is actually the kind of reasoning that has kept you in a condition of feeling the need.

Start little – purchase a companion an espresso; give a couple of coins to a busker or entertainer in the city; put your little change into a foundation tin or leave a tip where you may not normally do such an act. Search for other little approaches to part with a portion of the cash you have – you will have a positive outlook on doing it. Furthermore, this raises your vibration to be surer about cash.

These straightforward techniques will help you feel better about cash and lift your feelings. You are currently in the correct space to request that the Universe bring you more cash, permit yourself to get it, and be set up to make a move towards having more cash.

Cash isn't everything on the planet. There are different things more significant than money. The well-being, character, and conduct of the person are more significant than cash. It is appropriately stated, "Cash is lost, nothing is lost, well-being is lost, something is lost,, the character is lost, everything is lost". In this way, well-being also, the character is a higher priority than cash.

Other than that, the individual's character is most important. The individual who is benevolent and thoughtful to everybody is cherished by everyone and an individual who is egotistical or selfish is denounced by everyone. Yet, some eager individuals overlook all the imprudence and flaws of a well off individual. They are enticed to get cash from them. This compulsion to get the abundance of others. It is a negative way of generating cash and that too for the short-term. Ultimately, it drives us to pulverization.

We, individuals, don't have any affections for other people. Some of you might be exceptions. However, we should have a peaceful existence. We should not gain more money increasingly at the expense of others' lives. We give love and regard, as indicated by the measure of the quantity we have, and will get the money in return automatically.

Chapter 2:
Love

The most remarkable power on Earth, is love. It always reverberate what you want with adoration. At this point, the Law of attraction is a drop in the bucket that you hold. The fun thing about affection is that we are socially adapted to believe that 'love' signifies to clutch something. Whenever you experience passionate feelings and change for somebody, you need to wed them and be with them for the remainder of your life. You see something at the store that you love, and you need to take it home and own it. However, love can likewise be significantly communicated through giving up: releasing your youngster off to school, letting your companion has unexpected preferences in comparison to you, giving something that you treasure as a blessing to somebody you love. Taking everything into account, you grasp your cravings with adoration, and afterward, affectionately let go of them. While you can only hand it over to the Universe to be gotten back to you in the ideal impression of affection.

The Law of attraction has an amazing capacity to help you plan your fantasy love life. Regardless of whether you need to draw in more love into your life, fix the affection in your life, or any ork on your adoration life, the Law of attraction can help ou. It is incredible for those searching for help with family, companions, life partners, or others locally. As there are no limits on whom you can utilize the Law of appreciation to help you better your relationship with, expanding the measure of adoration and fondness that you feel for one another. Regardless of whether you are thinking about sentimental love, dispassionate love, or the sort of essential deference you feel for individuals in your day-to-day existence, for example, your colleagues or your chief, the Law of attraction can help you in these circumstances.

This part will investigate four significant adoration territories that the greater part of individuals might want to enhance. We will investigate how you can draw in affection, for example, through finding your perfect partner or getting your beau or sweetheart to propose to you, or in any event, winning your ex back. We will likewise talk about familial connections, including how you can mend connections among you and your family or improve them with the goal that the adoration you feel streams simpler for you. We will also talk about fellowships, including how you can draw in additional companions, have more grounded fellowships, or mend kinships that might be confronting hard times. At last, we will talk about how you can fix love, including how you can recuperate difficulties and contentions, conquer troublesome occasions, and in any case, mend a love that might be harmed among you and the individuals that you care about.

Before we start investigating these particular zones of adoration, how about we investigate how you can improve the adoration for your life by and large. This incorporates how you can experience more love from a more extensive perspective, including yourself and other people, and you and yourself. On the off chance that you need to experience and feel more love in your life and make the most of your life filled up with more love and warmth, you can make some fundamental changes that will help improve your odds, generally speaking. The accompanying six stages to love will help you go through the cycle of making schedules to assist you with pulling in adoration into your life as a rule. Request the affection you want, in any case. If you essentially need to feel more adore in your life, have better connections, or give love even more than before without restrictions, request this. Get explicit and request the entirety of your adoration life's territories that you need to be improved. This incorporates companions, family, your mate, colleagues, collaborators also, your chief, and with yourself. Get clear and centered, and make certain to ask routinely. Preferably, ask every day. Accept that you are commendable. Frequently, we battle to acknowledge the adoration we want into our lives since we feel ashamed of it. You need to dispense with these restricting convictions and start zeroing in on why individuals can adore you, not why they can't or shouldn't. You need to begin instructing yourself that you, and everybody else, are deserving of love. You have the right to be cherished; work towards accepting this day by day. Recuperate anything that you may have to defeat to respect this in yourself, and don't be reluctant to face the truth that you are loveable. The more you work on improving this aspect, better if you work on accepting this, the simpler it will be for you to both acknowledge and give love openly. Imagine what life will resemble when enhanced with the adoration you want. Envision the entirety of the manners in which our life will be upgraded or changed by the love you give and get. Set aside the effort to envision routinely exactly how much all that will change for you. What will it resemble for you to be cherished? What exactly would you feel like? How might your life look? Are you going to make more calls? Are you going to spend additional time with your friends and family, appreciating them and making the most of their presence? Will you pose basic inquiries like "how are you?" all the more frequently? Or, on the other hand, will you answer it with an all the more clear and genuine answer, as opposed to basic "I'm fine" answers that might be valid? How are you going to feel opening up in a more weak circumstance? Consider the entirety of your life's various ways that will be influenced and upgraded by affection and set aside the effort to consider how you react in these circumstances. Sincerely. Your reaction that you pick ought not to be quite the same as the one if you know who is that close person would be. You notice somebody adoring you for what your identity is; thus, you quit restoring their calls, picture what it resembles to pick up the telephone and speak with them all the more warmly concerning the kind of relationship you share. Imagine how your life will change routinely.

Act in arrangement with an individual who has a good love life. Buy a huge size bed and rest on one side with the goal that you are available to accepting somebody in your bed. Buy a giant couch or an extra guest plan for your home if you, at present, have a home that is more pointed toward a solitary individual.

Void a pull-out in your restroom or your bureau for somebody to use in your not so distant future. If it is a companionship that you are searching for, start closing off time on your timetable, where you will invest energy with companions. If you don't yet have companions, do it at any rate. Until you make companions, invest this energy calling family or friends and family, visiting regions where you may meet new individuals, or picturing what life will resemble when making new companions. Furthermore, open your time; heart up to get the affection you want through your activities. Get the adoration that you long for. This is the place where your conviction practices and mending practices will pay off. At the point when love begins showing up in your life, it is significant that you transparently get it. Try not to start to get apprehensive and permit old examples to settle in, persuading that you are shameful or that they are contemptible. Do not permit yourself to make distance and push them away, so you don't have to stay close to them. All things being equal, put time into making veritable and satisfying kinships. Put resources into the relationship as you need the other individual as well. If it turns out that they are not the right individual for you and the relationship normally closes, use it as a brilliant chance to figure out how you can remain open for suitable individuals to tag along. Try not to utilize it as proof to shut yourself off, accepting that you genuinely are shameful. This is ineffectual and will right away wipe out all the outcomes you have pursued.

Appreciation is consistently a significant piece of the training, as you most likely know! When it comes to cherishing, there are numerous brilliant and imaginative ways that you can communicate appreciation. Tell the individuals in your day-to-day existence that you care about them, that you love them, and that you are thankful for their kinship. Let your loved ones know that you love them and don't be reluctant to advise them routinely. If you have a contention or a spat, don't hesitate to share how you feel about it. Also, revive the relationship if you feel it is suitable to do. Keep in mind, everybody contends eventually. As you will find out about later in this area, numerous approaches to defeat these contentions with the goal that everybody included are regarded. Show appreciation at some random chance, and never be reluctant to impart your sentiments to other people straightforwardly. This weakness is where appreciation lies with regards to connections, both sentimental and nonromantic.

Love is a feeling everyone longs for. It makes them feel happy and important. It is often described as a warm and kind feeling that expresses affection. In a world where social problems are commonplace, if we love the little we can, we can solve most of them. While ongoing violence and other brutal, senseless murder only occur because people have forgotten about love, only negative thoughts are taught. Love is affection, and it can be said in many ways, and we should know that love hurts when shown or not shown in the right way. When we show love and care, we feel happy and content with life. Love is a universal theme, and it enriches our lives as we all have felt different kinds of love in our lives, where we experience negative thoughts. Our parents teach us to love in word, deed, and emotion with time we grew up. So it is the perfect truth and fact that when people say that love is life because life in some words without love would be mere life with no meaning. Love is seen in many aspects of our lives, as seen in literature, pop music, movies, religious literature, and the experiences of life.

In other words, love can be about family, partners, self, nature, and pets. Care and trust go hand in hand with affection. As individuals, we will, in general, be faithful to one another, and even though we might be unique, love joins us all and makes the world a superior spot.

Love is the most passionate experience we have when love and care show us. It's not simply dating. Loyalty, care, and trust build love. Everyone wants to be liked. It gives them pleasure and, besides, makes them happy and makes them feel special. We show care and love, which is around us, which can include everything around us, and the love we think of, is so much different throughout our lives.

Our first love experience was born. Father and mother love us from the moment we are in this world the day we are born, and this love between us expands. They show care for us and help us to improve. A child needs and deserves the warmth and love of his parents. So with time, we grow older and older, we learn a lot, and we learn to be independent with full liberty and not worry too much about our parents. Still, they are always available whenever we need them, and they will love us. If we keep it to negative thoughts, they will leave us, etcetera, but we cannot think in such a way, as we have hope in them, and they are there for us only. They care about us and make sure that we are always happy. As we get older and time passes, they teach us many principles, above all, about how to love. They love us, or we lead our lives, and they don't depend on them too much. The love for children from their parents is pure.

We show love to our siblings. Even though the brothers are fighting, they still love one another. Love is possible between two people caring for each other. Love can also be natural for us when we take care of plants and animals by protecting our environment.

It makes us content and makes us feel good. Showing love helps a person to feel better. Love is the foundation of any relationship we have in life.

Siblings and sisters may not generally coexist well with each other; however, their affection is excellent. Despite all the put-downs and contentions, they will consistently protect us. The adoration between them isn't spoken but it is felt; the outflow of affection isn't how we think it is. They love us no matter what.

Love is establishing a sentimental relationship; two mindful and cherishing accomplices. But they trust and believe each other and attempt to determine their disparities when they fight. Fellowship likewise has a subject of affection. They care about us, satisfy us, and care about us. Friendships dependent on affection and quality, which are rare, and this is why you should value them.

Companionship necessitates that you believe somebody you can open up to without reconsidering. She gains superb experiences and is upbeat. Everything considered, a companion and trustworthy person is somebody you can depend on; that is love. Here and there, this relationship may not work. Rather than feeling remorseful and embarrassed, we ought to like the occasions we have had and not disdain anybody. Love can be characteristic: acknowledging what the Earth has given us and protecting it with care.

Confidence is significant. When somebody accomplishes something else from what others see as typical, they will, in general, be forgotten about. Love isn't possessiveness. Individuals see reverence as ownership that ought to be obtained and guaranteed. To expect that others should offer it to us, so our life is piled up with fellowship is the best counterfeit thought, which clarifies much melancholy. Regardless of another person who offers us a huge adoration load, we will have no need for it.. It isn't appropriate to criticize others for not revering us. Love relies on our internal character, whether it can feel it from others.

Love is a propensity of flourishing and positive estimations. It is an improvement that keeps us in a fantastic soul and is gotten a kick out of the chance to our feelings. Grant us to draw in and establish a connection of worship by making self-fit through sensible changes in our dealings with others. There is no elective methodology to regard and be venerated. The genuine closeness without wonderful ideas isn't worshiped now need. Individuals are regularly negligent to imagine love as committed from an overall perspective. While guiding and looking at others, let us take care that our dealings make them euphoric by helping them with ascending out of their nervousness, regard their rewards, and be thankful for help gotten from them. The advantage of offering love to others is that it sells to our heart and makes us related to others, gives reliable quality and security, takes out dread, and gives a vibe of being sufficient towards others. One can get acquainted with adoration by first making such sensations in quite a while. Love is heavenly energy. I had an exceptionally dubious thought regarding love initially. I attempted to see more about it, an alternate point of view, and thinking build-up to clarify the genuine embodiment of affection. It shows up too theoretical in the primary occasion, yet more we will, in general, consider God will make us cherish God and any remaining manifestations of God. It resembles energy streaming inside us got from Ultimate that thinks positive and helps in internal cleansing. Scientists found that the energy-mass condition clarifies the interconnection of material and energy. It changed the present considering century by utilizing a limited quantity of mass to infer colossal energy. Subsequently, someplace, we are likewise important for the heavenly energy existing in us as torpid alongside our material presence. Intelligently, this heavenly energy, which is only loving, brings us near Ultimate. I can envision that all of us have an incredible limit of this heavenly love inside us. However, it is covered up, undiscovered, and misled. Incredible holy people have dealt with individuals now and again by creating an exceptional sensation of affection and worry for other people. This has helped them accomplish more significant levels of other worldly development and closeness with a definitive. The genuine importance of adoration is inward sanitization of the soul. This is a genuine reason for affection.

Love is only an internal need and the explanation behind inclination bliss. Fill the necessity of the soul by being enamored with another individual. The other individual to whom you love is just an item to be cherished; our feelings make love for that individual. Individuals love somebody if they feel that an individual is an adoration object. This understanding happens to inward needs. This explains that when the object of adoration is the same, various individuals respond to it alternately. An individual may turn into an object of affection for somebody. However, comparative sentiments might be absent in the core of another individual. The sensation of adoration lives in us; other individual turns out to be just a facilitator to draw out this inclination. Regardless of how great another individual might be, love should begin from you to make that caring feeling. Any remaining things follow from that point. These feelings come when we feel a need for adoration against negative feelings of outrage and scorn.

The benefits of offering affection to the next individual are basically to satisfy our internal needs and to produce satisfaction. Even if we request love from another individual, we will most likely be unable to feel it when our inward condition is loaded with negative sentiments. Love is a movement of pondering others, doing everything that could be done to cause others to feel better, and acting in a way that others feel good. It isn't something to be requested as it can't be protected, and we can't take it or feel it except if we make ourselves fit for it.

Everybody feels the effect of affection in their life. When you consider a great individual, you are in the same frequency as your internal identity, which causes you to feel light and upbeat. Such inclination is love. It is difficult for an individual to cherish somebody as it requires some investment to comprehend and afterward create loving of that individual.

Media impacts comprehension of different life issues, including an impression of adoration. Love has a diverse connotation in media, which isn't real. The individuals in love as shown in media are projected fairly exceptional; it makes us acknowledge unequipped for offering or getting such an adoration.

Individuals regularly revere affection, which is with no contention, loaded with penances and resistance from the other individual. The media praises love and show cherishing couple who do such countless strange things to draw in each other's' consideration. It influences the view of affection.

We envision ladies in affection as wonderful, forfeiting, and never contending. The media portrays love as dependent on actual attraction. In real life circumstance, things are unique. Love doesn't imply that there won't be any distinctions, and the other individual will consistently stay imbecilic. It doesn't imply that an individual not attractive or excellent will be less appealing and cherishing in nature. An individual's allure is portrayed from by and large character that is a mix of actual looks, uplifting disposition, and certainty. As reflected in media and described by different people, romantic tales generally describe the actual part of affection. It doesn't accentuate the passionate closeness and profound piece of the adoration, which is more inconspicuous and persevering. Our view of affection is, in this manner, restricted in nature.

Life isn't generally about the glad or tragic circumstances. It has its snapshots of ups and downs. Instructions to change in every circumstance and accept it will enormously influence the personal satisfaction and relationship with others. The view of adoration as being without any issue, inconvenience, and torment is hence misinterpretation. Individuals feel increasingly more agony as they can't live infatuated in relationship with others. Our impression of affection needs to change. We need to live with all the issues that we face as one, figure out our disparities, and change our way of life to bring similarity to adore and resistance in our disposition. We need to address the soul's issue to create profound love for different people, which goes past the actual attraction.

Individuals have created a lack of interest in others due to religion, social, public, financial contracts, and variations. This has made individuals loathe, and hearts are loaded up with awful emotions towards others. It influences producing a sensation of affection and closeness for other people. We stay indifferent about others; love and delicate emotions don't come effectively; we accept other people are unique and not near us.

The current climate isn't helpful, and in these conditions, exceptional endeavors like cleaning of heart from terrible emotions towards others, are required. It requires a certified adoration sensation, love, and worry for other people. Barely any incredible character right now, either in the social or political field lectures general love and fraternity. Countries and social orders lay a lot of significance on material accomplishments, while these elusive advantages, which are ideal for enduring satisfaction, are overlooked. Quite a bit of our consideration through books, lecturing, and media regarding material government assistance, Youngsters, understudies, and collect data on different fields; however, an infrequently instructive educational plan lays significance on human qualities dependent on adoration and friendship. It has made individuals dismiss great estimations of life based on adoration and sympathy. Individuals measure accomplishment with the measuring stick of material solaces. Life has gotten uneven as this urgent part of our need isn't completely stressed.

A large portion of us appends such countless conditions to have the option to cherish and like another individual. We expect that other individuals should merit love from us. This weakens our ability to cherish somebody who needs it most. As individuals become increasingly complex and refined in their quest for material solaces, they will, in general, miss the mark in their ability to cherish others. They find another individual not proficient and refined and feel it hard to cherish and show positive sentiments. The genuine romance necessitates that it should not to be contingent. Love should stream out of empathy for another individual. Our hearts should create a sensation of adoration and concern. Love in the unadulterated structure implies offering without expecting anything as a trade-off. This is a genuine romance. At the point when the mother loves kids, it is unqualified and is unadulterated. The mother feels inconvenience in taking care of the kid; notwithstanding, she has an internal inclination to address all the kid's issues and considers the young kid as her bliss.

The ability to adore is affected if we generally hope to get something from others consequently. Internal identity needs adequate sensations of affection and worry for another individual. If we consider offering something to others in affection, it necessitates that we are happy with what we have had. It helps produce love for other people if we are quiet and content with ourselves. An individual's limit to give something in affection doesn't generally rely upon their material effects; however, the eagerness and character of that individual. Giving something doesn't mean contributing just material belongings. If an individual has the readiness to give something valuable to other people, the person in question can cherish others. When we consider providing for another individual, we care for that individual. It offers a word of wisdom, acclaims, certified compassion, or whatever other assistance that he/she needs at that material time. When a mother or father cherishes a kid, they are dealing with the youngster.

Love goes with care, empathy, and resilience. These characteristics are to be created to produce love for another individual. This requires a change in our demeanor to life. The endeavors that go with growing such characteristics help an individual advance his existence with positive energy.

It isn't unexpected to be occupied about own material achievement, force, and distinction, and in the process do little to grow genuine sensation of affection. In general, we will cause another individual to accept that we love that person, yet might be missing internal inclination of worry for that individual. It is common with so many of us to feel ardent of a dear companion or relative. These negative inclinations continue frequenting us that influences genuinely adorable inclination. Individuals become pessimists of others and attempt to discover flaws.

In some cases, they feel miserable to discover another individual better positioned throughout everyday life. It is complex to create the sensation of affection for another individual except if we dispose of these negative perspectives. The best approach to sticking to virtues is to think and work for others' good. When we attempt to stay great to other people, it creates an inward sensation of adoration and warmth. Consider adoring others much as we love ourselves.

Personality and egotistical sentiments come in the manner to produce a sensation of adoration and empathy for another individual. So, if an individual is effective in their calling, it needs not to build up a sensation of affection and sympathy for other people. Achievement and abundance may turn an individual self-absorbed and think that it's hard to acknowledge others as equivalent. The second we feel higher than others, it makes us hope for something else in affection and dutifulness from others, than we give as a trade-off. The ability to cherish others gets influenced whenever loaded up with such sentiments. Out of a feeling of inadequacy, different people may regard us, yet it will be shy of producing adoring sentiments in their hearts. We set a cap for genuine romance by carrying these negative feelings loaded with our sense of self and dominance. It requires some investment and genuine endeavors to clean these emotions.

Individuals regularly assume that they love another individual; however, they are ignorant of whether such sentiments are passed on in the way other individuals see it. It demonstrates the absence of affectability to communicate sensations of adoration. What is the point in professing to be enamored with another individual on the off chance that you neglect to get such emotions from other individuals?

Love is a method for correspondence of positive sentiments to the next individual. It is the wish for assistance, achievement, and joy of an individual. These emotions create when we love an individual. It makes us aware that our activities will cause another individual to feel good. Express sentiments to an individual in a manner it matches his/her affectability. Lovemaking is an individual issue, and every individual might want to feel about adoration in a specific way. Love requests enthusiastic closeness through consideration, sympathy, resilience, and comprehension,

Affectability is towards a specific way we talk, express our sentiments, and comprehend another individual. If we deal with another individual's affectability in these issues, it will help in more agreeable connections and better-shared arrangements. Sensations of adoration get impeded if we don't talk pleasantly to other people and attempt to prod or discover flaws. Be careful while talking so that we don't hurt another individual in any capacity. There will be several events in our day-to-day existence when we will vary from others. If an individual out of personality carries on prevalent, it causes another individual to feel little and hurt.

Love is inconspicuous, and it doesn't have quick unmistakable advantages. We need certain changes to build up a sensation of affection and worry for other people. These emotions come, we esteem support of others as significant as our own, which is reflected in our disposition towards others. A few people by heart are accommodating and supportive of other people— individuals who see self interest more significant set aside some effort to build up these better characteristics. What we anticipate from life coordinates our reactions and dealings with others. Aside from how others treat us, our internal urge drives us to feel love and worry for others.

We frequently discover couples portraying love towards one another in others' presence by regularly embracing and kissing. Individuals state 'I Love You' time and again to others around them, yet need to discover inside whether they are consistent with their promise. To communicate love just through words isn't adequate. It must be portrayed in real life. In some cases, we don't know of our adoration towards others but rather rehash these uplifting statements to fulfill that individual.

The love of a mother for the youngsters illustrates the unobtrusive adoration type. She will attempt to shield the youngster from all the odds. She won't abandon the youngster if not doing admirably throughout everyday life. Outside components don't restrict her adoration. If the kid is tricky, she will keep dealing with the youngster. She is touchy to the sensations of the kid.

In genuine affection towards another individual, it includes outright honesty unafraid of misdirection. This requires genuineness with the other individual. Accept something about the individual yet express it distinctively shows the absence of genuineness. When we manage the individual, the brain and heart must be as one to receive trustworthiness in our idea and deeds. In managing others, we are impacted by our sensations of adoration and warmth produced through our heart while our brain esteems the relationship dependent on common advantage. It gets a matter of internal clash, as we should give in a connection and the amount to get. Now and again, whatever we express may not be essential to what we feel about the individual. Our relationship now and again needs affectability, which influences genuine romance.

To be fascinated with others is the need for the soul; the same as food is our body's need. We generally feel inclined to associate with the other individual through adoration and sensation of closeness. Getting physically and personally involved with others doesn't mean actual closeness, yet it includes more extensive importance of better comprehension through adoration and sympathy. Closeness necessitates that we open our hearts and fill them with affection for the other soul. Love others as your perfect partners to be in a genuine romance with the other individual.

There is not an individual who might never need to feel cherished. In any case, once there is a mindful individual by the side, love is by all accounts a figment as opposed to a reality. The question here is the meaning of affection. It is still unknown whether love holds its importance for the individual or it is just the manifestation. Love is an endless, unqualified state as it is set up by singular decision, exacting both positive and negative outcomes.

Essentially, love isn't an inclination. It might appear to be that we experience passionate feelings dependent on our feelings. Such cases as unexplainable adoration are regularly guided by fast, passionate association with an alternate individual. Nonetheless, genuine love is a perspective, as it an aftereffect of an individual decision to tie your existence with another person. Emotions are tagging along, for example, attraction, bliss, or joy. Nevertheless, real love will exceed the enthusiastic conditions, understanding the individual's downsides as opposed to assessing benefits.

Furthermore, love is unceasing, just like a genuine state. This implies that connections will be solid restricting individuals together once the decision is made. When individuals live with one another for quite a while, sharing considerations and difficulties of life, the underlying emotions dissipate. It is love that keeps two various people together and makes them look for bargains to bring back the emotions.

Finally, love holds both positive and negative ramifications for a person. Settling on adoring, someone can cause colossal joy that will last every day. In any case, connections infer happiness,. But if there are confusions in the decisions, it will uncover an alternate individual's disadvantages. In such a condition, love can be dismissed, as one individual would be hesitant to settle on a similar decision for the all-around settled person.

Love isn't only a topic in films and writing, yet it is the most extreme emotion of our daily life. With a firm feeling of adoration estimation, every single one of us is fit for appearing, pulling in, and looking after affection. Love is joined by an equity cognizance that encourages self-strengthening and doesn't zero in just on the quick hover of loved ones. Love resembles a rose, the excellence of affection can't be portrayed, yet its stems are loaded up with thistles. The above articles and film transformations have indicated that affection accompanies envy, scorn, and clashes. However, that ought not to make us abandon love.

Chapter 3:
Power

The information on the Law of Attraction causes us to be enlightened about how all that is occurring in our lives is just the aftereffect of what we are continually feeling and thinking. This reality can free us from an aloof spectator's situation to a proactive one.

An individual with a negative demeanor towards life awakens and sees just antagonism in general. He sees that terrible things are going on to him and may even feel reviled. Yet, the Law of Attraction discloses that we can deliberately pick our background, and by deduction and empathetic feeling, we can improve our real factors. It doesn't make a difference where you were born, how much cash your family has, regardless of whether you were acceptable in school or even if you were brought into the world without any legs and arms.

Everybody was brought into the world with The Law of Attraction, and it works the equivalent for all of humanity.

There are a few things that we can't change, for example, you were conceived without any legs and no arms. You can't just develop them. Nonetheless, individuals who were naturally

Julia Meadows

introduced to comparative conditions such as this one can at present benefit as much as possible from what he has been given. By utilizing The Law of Attraction, we are, for the most part, similarly as capable as any other to make the way of life we had always wanted.

The Law of Attraction works through the intensity of core interest. As you move your concentration from negative to positive, you begin to change the encounters and change your life. You might be an individual who has no clue about what the Law is, or you might be an individual who realizes a little about how the law functions or you might be somebody who has just made some progress by executing the Law's standards in your everyday life.

Power fundamentally radiates from a position of authority, impacting individuals both emphatically and awkwardly. Having an inspirational disposition is about more than putting a grin all over; it implies development of the gradual feeling of thankfulness for what you now have and for what you expect will come. Move your concentration from what you believe you need toward sensations of appreciation and wealth.

Likewise, you can fortify your inspirational outlook by sharing your objectives, dreams, and goals with others. Spreading your inspiration to your friends and family additionally permits you to get and give uphold. Force has been a significant part of human development since yore days. Force may be physical, political, or social. The force depends on individual to individual, and its utilization relies on the demeanor of a person. Force in open life is not the same as in the corporate world. While the previous is situational, the last is the object arranged. In open life, its guarantees could conceivably function as wanted.

Legitimate utilization of force in the association is essential, so the wellsprings of intensity aren't abused and coordinated towards fulfilling the authoritative objective. It is critical to comprehend the administrator who uses the capacity to comprehend representative conduct since strategies for utilizing power are distinctive for different associations.

Along these lines, it is basic to permit the least power that might be important to keep up the tranquil climate. The investigation to see how power is gained and utilized to achieve hierarchical objectives is basic. Regarding business also, power elements will, in general, impact choices and individuals exchanges intensely. So characterizing force can be troublesome as it is perceived and deciphered severely. In anyway force cannot be known as a power that gets you what you need. Force essentially exudes from an authority, which can impact individuals both positively and adversely.

Along these lines, the force can be characterized in various ways; anyway, what is significant is the force's use by individuals who have it. Inside the authoritative setting, the force elements and conditions should be deliberately overseen as they hugely affect workers' inspiration and commitment level. It additionally characterizes the association's way of life when all is said in practical and individuals deal inside the association specifically. A very chain of importance and force-driven association thinks it's hard to oblige new and inventive thoughts. Any change is intense. can't, inner selves conflict, and lesser chances are made accessible for the superior workers, accordingly deferring authoritative development. Then again, at an association level in the structure, individuals are urged to enhance and investigate, accordingly acquiring new ideas and thoughts to quicken hierarchical development and extension.

Words are viewed as a puzzling creation of correspondence in our regular day-to-day existence. Forces of picked words have the ability to advise, impact, teach and engage others. Words can summon rich pictures of inward and external feelings through various correspondence methods. Their forces are communicated successfully and sincerely in stories, sonnets, papers, fine arts, and so on. Words are the most impressive medication utilized by humankind. Words are what we use to communicate ourselves, our contemplations, and our emotions. We use words in each stroll of our lives, and henceforth the intensity of these words is tremendous and incredible. The effect of words on various individuals differs since it relies upon their arrangement and how they imagine it. Overall, when individuals need to impart and communicate, they use words, the most impressive medication. Words can impact us from numerous points of view, such as satisfying us, making us tragic, enthusiastic, and so forth, and have swayed on us from various perspectives, for example, affecting and evolving lives. This is the place where the story "Two Words" holds significance. As words, regardless of how much of the time we use, hold incredible significance because they can shape lives, and makes us consider upon. Words are a crucial adornment of endurance in this day and age, and they are communicated diversely in and several styles, which everybody needs to learn to comprehend its significance.

We all wish to accomplish numerous things throughout everyday life. Yet, generally, a considerable lot of us don't prevail with regards to accomplishing anything. What's even worse? We will regularly revile our destiny, or incidents in general. However, the truth is that we have just ourselves to fault for our disappointments. Is there such an incredible concept as fate? If our Will-Power is strong, we can, without a doubt, overcome all impediments. The possibility of fate is human-made. It isn't adequate that we wish to achieve something. We should have the fitting discretion to do our planes.

Indeed, even a superficial investigation of human progress's historical backdrop reveals to us that men will have consistently accomplished all incredible things. Incredible men become extraordinary since the very start, and they had willed to be extraordinary. The prominent accomplishments of science, artistry, and writing are, for the most part, the consequence of attempts of MEN OF WILL who neutralized hefty chances to accomplish their objectives.

Without such assurance, we won't place enough solidarity to make our arrangement a triumph. Aside from that, in any event, when the overall look of our plan looks dull, we will pay special attention to minor details for progress. Even a decent plan with enough scale won't succeed if there is the absence of WILL. What makes a difference is that we have the legitimate drive or assurance to continue with our plans despite snags.

A couple of models would do the trick to express the idea effectively. Columbus could find America simply because he stood firm against all the tempests of challenges that would have compromised him. Nothing could discourage him from the way that he had decided for himself. Madam Curie could find Radium - an incredible aid to humanity - simply because they were people of WILL arranged to set down even their lives chasing their ideal.

Like Napoleon, incredible victors were all men of assurance who will constrain conveyed everything before it. Coming closer home, we get the motivating illustration of Hillary and Tensing, who remained against all the threats of high heights in their purpose to arrive at the highest point of Everest. Encouraged by enormous WILL-FORCE, Gandhi exhibited to the world definitively that it is WILL that matters and not the physical condition.

WILL is an incredible power, both for good and malevolence. It makes outlandish things conceivable. The tale of man's advancement from disarray to arrange, from boorishness to progress, is only an account of his WILL POWER set in opposition to all the unfriendly powers of nature. This WILL POWER can be accomplished by any of us by the nonstop cycle of fixation on respectable goals. When procured, it will empower us to have our way no matter what.

Power is a tool and resource, and a means for an end. The politics in an organizational setting represents tactics used by employees to manipulate power in an organizational setting.

A superior may utilize corrective ability to keep a person from limiting errant activities. The manager who has the power to promote his subordinates uses it to attain organizational goals. Power should be used to attain the organization's growth and should be reward oriented in nature. The danger of force isn't alluring as it has a negative re-implementation character inbuilt in it.

At the point when we examine power, authority is related to it. Authority is gained from the hierarchical chain of command. When we state that the HR chief can utilize an individual, this authority is related to an HR supervisor's arrangement.

It is, therefore, legitimate. Authority relationship of the various individual is contained in the organizational pyramid chart. The higher one goes with the higher the authority. Authority and force go connected.. To be successful, force and authority ought to be leveled.

Authority and force are interchangeable. In any case, in the current climate, it is seen that while authority stays consistent, there is a propensity to practice more power. This results from a person's issues to keep a more grounded impact over the resources. Despite what might be expected, there might be circumstances when an individual doesn't utilize his position's maximum capacity for one explanation or the other.

Interpersonal and group conflicts indicate more influence one wants to exercise in the organizational setting. These happening are common to every layer of the organizational hierarchy. Power is, therefore, personal and acquired. Force is the capacity of an individual to have what he feels as important and deny someone else.

As indicated by Wolfe, power is the likely capacity of an individual to actuate powers on someone else towards development or alter in a given course inside a given conduct district at a given time. Cavanaugh2 states that 'Force' is a multifaceted idea, which has been examined from the relational impact measure, as a product to be exchanged, as a sort of causation, and as an issue in investigating qualities and morals.

Politics is a process whereby power is acquired and used to influence others' behavior. It is endemic to every organization. People form groups, camps, or cliques when they play politics. People are playing politics for power where ethics, moral values, organizational goals are of little concern.

The relationship between force and confidence is most likely a consequence of their proportional impacts. From one perspective, increased confidence may prepare to control. To accomplish power, people need to have confidence in their ability and deservingness to do as such, and high confidence is by all accounts an essential of such convictions. Then again, varieties in force may impact confidence, and this is the experimental focal point of studies detailed beneath. Our fundamental postulation is that uplifted force builds confidence while excessive power drives down to diminish the confidence. This speculation can be gotten from the methodology hindrance hypothesis of force (Keltner et al., 2003), which expects that raised force implies admittance to assets (both material and mental) and absence of social and regularizing imperatives, along these lines enacts an overall methodology framework. The methodology framework includes appetitive cycles related to objective achievement, positive effect, and expanded affectability to rewards (Gray, 1994). Diminished force implies an absence of assets and coercion to social requirements, subsequently initiating an overall hindrance framework. The hindrance framework includes evasion or reaction restraint inclinations related to negative effects and elevated watchfulness and discipline examination. An expanding measure of experimental examination shows significant contrasts in individuals' feelings, psychological, and conduct working supplied with high versus low force. Predictable with the methodology framework actuation approach, individuals high in force experience more certain and more positive feelings and are bound to see rewards.

The main kind of intensity is an authentic force or "positional force," it has a place with a person because of his position in the public arena and his obligations. He is to perform there. The genuine force is that power designated to someone by the specialists. It very well may be upheld by various extra credits, for example, uniform, title, and so on. Referent force is the second sort of intensity available when an individual can pull in others, fabricating a sort of reliability and attraction. For this situation, the power holder ought to have individual magnetism and certain abilities to acquire and keep up his capacity. This individual may have one solid individual attribute, which would pull in individuals around him, and they likewise need to distinguish them with this quality. The most splendid referent force instances are energy or patriotism when troopers are anxious to battle to ensure safety for their nation. In the present day, business sponsors utilize the referent force to pull in new clients when they allude to celebrated games stars, for instance, or vocalists, utilizing their Moxy and public appreciation. One of the critical qualities of referent force is its absence of dependability. Hence this is a terrible choice for the pioneer, looking for long regard and backing. It could likewise be joined with different wellsprings of intensity and, afterward, be fairly effective.

Master power is regularly present in associations, having a place with a person who has high abilities and experience and can compare to the association's necessities. One of the disadvantages of this force is that it is explicit; as such, it has a place just within the boundary in which this individual is prepared and is a trained professionally.

They talked about remuneration power again, which is a sort of intensity, which depends on the material prizes, which could be given by the person who packs it in his grasp. These could be blessings, benefits, advancements, the increment of pay, etc. This force isn't that hard to acquire. Anyway, it might be good, but effectively lost. The issues start when the individual, having this force, begins to manhandle it or plays a round of having it without having it in all actuality. For instance, if an individual has a fairly high situation in an association, this doesn't imply that he has total tons of his subordinates. There is consistently a top managerial staff, which takes key official choices, and when this becomes clear, an individual can't have this sort of intensity so solid. The contrary sort of remuneration power is coercive force. It depends on a person's capacity to retain, compensate, or deny others of something. This force isn't that viable as it normally needs to confront encounters and opposition from the side of individuals who wind up under it. The most usually applied apparatuses of coercive force are discipline and dangers, which could be various. Individuals could be taking steps to lose their employment, their advantages, get an unpleasant work assignment, and so on.

Typically, this sort of intensity is related to the ruined administration style.

For many years, for ages, individuals needed to have control and impact since they were persuaded that these two perspectives would give admittance to endless capacity to them. On the opposite, holding onto power was the fundamental point since it could impact others, their activities, and their choices. As yet contemplating that everything in this world is interrelated, it is absurd to expect to have outright force or supreme power over anything.

Chapter.4:
Happiness

Happiness can mean various things to individuals. I, for instance, absolutely never get euphorically upbeat, which could possibly be your meaning of satisfaction. However, I can witness something superb, and tears will move down my face. And afterward, on occasion, I can be truly cheerful. So Bliss can be a wide reach for me. In any case, the condition of satisfaction is a decision and should be found where you are present.

We are socially molded to look for Bliss from things outside of ourselves: in the companions we have, the vehicle we drive, the in-vogue garments we wear, the victories we accomplish, the house we occupy, and additionally the cash we have in the bank. In this manner, most of us keep holding up through every snapshot of our lives for our external conditions to fulfill us: for better well-being, a more appealing body, a caring relationship, a better work, etc. But, in this manner, we confound the circumstances and logical results of how things truly work. It is the Bliss that creates our great encounters, not the opposite way around. The Law of Attraction it wouldn't work if it were some other way.

Happiness is the belief that comes over you when you realize life is acceptable, and you can't resist the urge to grin. Joy is the condition of passionate prosperity and being placated. Happiness is communicated through upbeat minutes and grins. It is an alluring inclination that everyone needs to have consistently. Being upbeat is impacted by circumstances, accomplishments, and different conditions. Happiness is an inward quality that considers the perspective. A serene perspective is viewed as Bliss. The passionate condition of Bliss is a combination of sensations of Happiness, fulfillment, appreciation, elation, and triumph. Bliss varies from individual to individual; various individuals have various discernments and originations of being cheerful. Whatever that might be, Bliss is a fundamental component of human existence. Without it, life holds no importance by any means. It is beyond the realm of the imagination at all for an individual to carry on with their lives without Happiness and Bliss. Joy is unexpectedly characterized by various feelings. At the point when we feel good feelings, we will, in general, feel glad. That is what is the issue here. Happiness is additionally viewed as the psychological condition of an individual in a hopeful way. Bliss is a perspective, and the inclination communicated when things are going extraordinary. It is the thing that we feel when we get our first vehicle, purchase another house, or graduate with the best grades. Joy ought to be recognized from delight. At the point when Bliss is a consistent perspective, joy relies upon occasions in our lives.

The vast majority accept that Bliss is equivalent to satisfaction, yet individuals don't persuade the alternative to be upbeat. This is one of the numerous reasons that Bliss isn't related to Happiness. You don't should be glad to be euphoric because Euphoria is a mentality; it did not depend on feelings and is lasting and comes from inside. While a large number of us consider Euphoria bliss, Happiness is not a mentality. Happiness is a decision and attitude. Each individual characterizes satisfaction in his/her own way. In whatever way you may characterize happiness, in all actuality, it is indispensable for a sound and prosperous life.

Genuine Bliss implies the fulfillment that you discover commendable. The dependable, genuine Bliss comes from life experience, a sensation of direction, and a positive relationship. Happiness is something that we can't depict in words. It must be felt from somebody's appearance of a grin. Similarly, satisfaction is a sign or ID of a good and prosperous life. Bliss is extremely easy to feel and hard to depict. Besides, satisfaction comes from the inside, and nobody can take your joy. The joy of the psyche is frequently viewed in opposition to envy and outrage, which you experience whenever you have fizzled or unaccomplished any ideal objective. You ought to consistently attempt to practice the methods of keeping yourself fulfilled and avoiding pessimism to encounter harmony and Bliss throughout everyday life. Genuine Bliss starts where want closes.

Satisfaction is accomplished mentally by having a quiet perspective. From a free perspective, I imply that there ought to be no distressing elements to consider. Satisfaction is likewise accomplished through the achievement of objectives that are set by people. There is consistently Bliss that goes with progress, and they present sensations of win and Happiness.

To empower individual Happiness throughout everyday life, it is significant that an individual puts himself first and has great self-insight. Putting what fulfills you first, rather than putting others or different things initially, is a genuine journey towards Bliss. Throughout everyday life, individuals will, , frustrate. Putting them as a need consistently decreases Bliss for people. There is additionally the idea of rehearsing confidence and self-acknowledgment. Cherishing oneself is the way to bliss since it will imply that it won't be difficult to put yourself first when deciding.

It is significant for a person to control the musings that go on in their minds. A serene perspective is accomplished when considerations find a sense of contentment. It is suggested that things that cause a distressing perspective ought to be dodged.

Bliss is an individual choice that is impacted by decisions made. There is a typical expression of Happiness; "joy is a decision," which is exceptionally evident because individuals pick if they need to be cheerful or not. Happiness is brought about by conditions, and individuals have the freedom to pick that situation and move away from those that make them miserable.

Bliss is additionally accomplished through the emotionally supportive network that an individual has. Having a family or companions that are strong will empower the accomplishment of joy. Conveying and cooperating with the rest of the world is significant.

Rest schedules impact the perspective which ultimately reflects in the joy. Having enough rest consistently prompts upbeat mornings and a decent perspective for the rest of the day. Rest that is sufficient likewise influences the presence of an individual. There is the fulfillment that accompanies having enough rest. Enough rest builds execution and efficiency of an individual, and consequently, more triumphs and accomplishments are acknowledged, and joy is capable.

Another factor influencing joy is the encouraging group of people of a person. A solid, encouraging group of people of loved ones brings about more joy. Setting up great associations with neighbors, loved ones through customary collaborations carries more joy to a person. With an encouraging group of people, the occurrences of upsetting minutes will be decreased because your loved ones will consistently be of help.

Sexual fulfillment has been set up to influence joy. It isn't just about getting the correct accomplice any longer. It is tied in with having an accomplice that will fulfill you explicitly. There is a connection between sex and Bliss due to the chemicals discharged during sex. The chemical is called oxytocin and liable for the joy because of sexual fulfillment. Fulfillment additionally fortifies the connections between the accomplices, and that makes Bliss.

Abundance likewise assumes a huge job in satisfaction. There is a typical expression that is against cash and Bliss: "Money can't buy happiness" is this valid? Actually, I accept that being monetarily steady adds to satisfaction since you will consistently have significant serenity and numerous accomplishments. True serenity is workable for rich individuals since they don't have stressors here in comparison with needy individuals. Additionally, when an individual is rich, they can stand to take part in lavish exercises that loosen up the mind and make Bliss. For an individual to be well off, they will have had numerous accomplishments throughout everyday life. These accomplishments satisfy them.

A decent condition of well-being is a significant factor that impacts the joy of people. A sound individual will be cheerful because there are no concerns about sicknesses or torment that they are encountering. At the point when an individual is sound, their perspective finds a sense of contentment since they are not terrified of death or some other well-being concerns. The well-being of people is significant, yet additionally, the soundness of the emotionally supportive network of the individual. Loved one's condition of well-being will consistently affect what we feel as people since we care about them, and we get stressed at whatever point they have terrible well-being.

Correspondence and connections are significantly comparable to a person's satisfaction. Having an emotionally supportive network isn't sufficient because individuals need to convey and interface unreservedly. There are co-operations like a get-together where individuals talk and eat together, to get the inherent bliss. This idea is seen in gatherings since individuals are continually chuckling and grinning in gatherings at whatever point they are with companions.

Openness is absolutely vital for satisfaction since it helps in critical thinking and easing stressors throughout everyday life.

Sharing with an emotionally supportive network helps in betterment. At some point when I am pitiful, I take my telephone and call a companion or a relative, and when the call is finished, I generally feel much improved and alleviated of my concerns.

Joy is emotional. There is nobody manner by which the term can be characterized. For various individuals, Happiness holds various undertones. It infers a perspective; for other people, it may mean a norm of the way of life. Every person is an autonomous, free-thinking person. Everybody has a point of view that is not quite the same as the other. Consequently, the meaning of Happiness is likewise an individual characteristic. In any case, whatever might be Happiness's meaning, there is no rejecting that Happiness is a basic piece of our lives. There is no reason for living or going about throughout everyday life without it.

The expression that we have been talking about: "Money can't buy happiness", somewhat, it tends to be proclaimed as legitimate. Nonetheless, a few people may discover it to be bogus. For a particular segment of society, Happiness is characterized by abundance. In general, these individuals will consider abundance as the estimating pole for their delights throughout everyday life. So for others, it is true that pleasure and enjoyment in life come from material belonging and prosperity. Wealth, cash, gems, gold, and abundance fulfill them; they stay content with these in their lives.

For another part of society, abundance doesn't go about the driving force for Happiness in their lives. Many believe Happiness is a tranquil and quiet feeling of delight inside one's brain. For them, it can't be estimated as far as common things. In general, Joy will turn into an inclination that can be gotten a handle on through the fulfillment of the psyche and soul and not through the delight of the body. Satisfaction, for a few, can likewise suggest achievement. Being dedicated, and effective frequently become manners by which an individual gets Happiness throughout everyday life.

Whatever be our modes and strategies for getting cheerful, it will, in general, continue to change over the long haul. No inclination is total. It may happen that the things used to make us open to during our youth; at this point, don't hold similar importance in our lives. This happens because our needs and objectives change over the long run.

Consequently, the condition of being glad to a great extent relies on what a specific individual needs from life. It relies on an individual's longings and objectives throughout everyday life. Most importantly and much of the time, enjoying the things that one loves the most turns into the way into a cheerful life.

Thus, love and Happiness are straightforwardly connected. Without affection, Happiness doesn't persevere. Moreover, without Happiness, love doesn't persevere.

As referenced, a collection of things fulfills happiness for different individuals. There is no correct method to acquire Happiness. Various individuals have various techniques by which they can determine Happiness. Every one of them is substantial; none of them is bogus or off base. Deciding individuals dependent on what they love and what they scorn isn't reasonable. As a whole, we have various needs throughout everyday life, and not those are comparative. They can be unique, yet that doesn't mean they are incorrect. Doing whatever fulfills one feel back to front ought to be viewed as legitimate and legitimate.

Reliably we see and meet people who look happy about an outside perspective, anyway where it really matters, and they are broken and miserable from the inside. For certain people, money is an essential driver of Happiness or misery. However, this doesn't appear to be correct. Money can get you food, a rich house, strong lifestyle laborers, and many more workplaces, yet money can't get you satisfaction.

What is the cash could have purchased you joy? At that point, the rich would be the most joyful individual on the earth. But, we see an opposite picture of the rich as they are miserable, unfortunate, restless, focused, and experiencing different issues. The poor are more joyful than the rich; yet on the off chance that we talk about abundance, the rich are more well off, at that point, poor people. Moreover, abundance brings weakness, uneasiness, and numerous different issues. Besides, they have cash still, and they need a public activity with their family, particularly their spouses, which is the fundamental driver of separation.

Likewise, because of cash, they feel insecure. They feel that everybody is after their cash to protect their cash and enlist security. At the same time, the poor state is the exact inverse. They don't have cash, yet they are content with and tranquil from these issues. Furthermore, they deal with their significant other and youngsters, and their separation rate is additionally meager. As we presently realize that we can't accept satisfaction with cash, and there is no other alternate route to joy. It is something that you feel from the inside.

Moreover, genuine joy comes from inside you. Bliss is fundamentally a perspective. Additionally, it must be accomplished by being positive and maintaining a strategic distance from any negative idea as a primary concern. Additionally, if we take a gander at the splendid side of ourselves in particular, at that point, we can be glad.

Individuals these days are not happy with their relationship due to their disparities and many other explanations. In any case, for being upbeat in a relationship, we need to comprehend that there are a few principles or shared agreement that keeps a relationship solid and glad. Right off the bat, deal with yourself then your accomplice. Supposing that you, when all is said and done, are distressed and this is how you are going to see your partner, creating even more problems once you'll get back to your normal position.

Besides, a cheerful and sound relationship gives your accomplice some idea about your personality. Moreover, attempt to comprehend their inclination and solace level. But when in rage, you don't comprehend these things. You won't have the option to comprehend your accomplice appropriately.

Above all, step up and plan to go out with your accomplice and family. Furthermore, if they have plans, at that point, go with them. To close, we can say that satisfaction must be accomplished by having positive reasoning and appreciating life. Likewise, for being glad and keeping the individuals around us happy, we need to build a solid relationship with them. Furthermore, we additionally need to give them the appropriate time. When joined into our everyday lives, there are little things that can lead us to the way of joy. For example, rather than considering issues, we ought to really be pondering the arrangements. We be more joyful, yet we will likewise have the option to tackle our issues quicker. Additionally, on occasion, you start the day with the aching to accomplish a couple of targets. At the day's end, you may feel frustrated and hopeless, considering the way that you haven't had the ability to do those things. Investigate what you have done, not at what you have not had the ability to do. Routinely, whether or not you have accomplished a ton by the end of the day, you let yourself feel frustrated because of some minor tasks you didn't accomplish. This removes satisfaction from you.

Once more, every so often, you finish your day successfully finishing various plans, yet instead of feeling merry and satisfied, you see what you left and feel upset. It is off the mark towards you. Every day achieves something great which you appreciate doing. In general, it might be something little, for example, buying a book, eating something you esteem, seeing your most adored program on TV, taking off to a film, or just having a stroll around the beach. Indeed, even little things can get incredible degrees of joy in our lives and persuade us for new objectives.

Joy isn't what you feel from outside. And rather, it comes from your inward soul. We should discover the joy in us instead of looking for it in common longings. Carry Bliss and profound life to yourself instead of anticipating it from the rest of the world like things, cash, and so on. Being cheerful isn't as simple as encouraged to be one more joyful individual. To be content and content with whatever you have and yourself requires some investment and persistence. It would help if you practiced being a more joyful individual in all minutes, and at last, you will see that no distress can sink you.

Whatever positive or negative occurred in your past shouldn't trouble your present. Figure out how to live today with more Bliss than yesterday and disregard your previous pity for an amicable life. Gratefulness to the existence you got is another significant character you ought to obtain to be happy. If you contrast yourself and somebody with better extravagant life, at that point, you won't ever be glad or content, rather sad and complaining. Try not to push down your brain with awful and negative considerations about yourself and around. Attempt to discover each truth in a circumstance you confront and acknowledge the things that all around occurred, regardless of whether fortunate or unfortunate. Remember to pick merrier and positive individuals to be nearer to you, so their vibes will help you be one merrier individual.

At whatever point you feel low and discouraged, never wonder whether or not to go to people around you to discover joy. However, know about those negative ones that may maneuver you significantly into the awful musings. Continuously encircle yourself with positive reasoning and inspiring individuals so you can ascend higher even from the most profound fall. Satisfaction is only an inclination that will be cultivated into your spirit just if you wish to, and nothing other than yourself can enjoy this inclination in you. Try not to ruin your life discovering satisfaction elsewhere.

Joy is something muddled. Satisfaction can be utilized both in an enthusiastic or mental state setting and can generally fluctuate from an inclination from Happiness to the exceptional sensation of delight. It can likewise mean a day-to-day existence of fulfillment, great prosperity thus some more. Bliss is an exceptionally troublesome if you want to utilize words to portray as it is something that can be felt not said. Joy is significant to lead an awesome life. Tragically, Bliss is missing from the lives of many individuals these days. As a whole, we have our own altogether different idea of satisfaction. A few of us are aware that we can get Bliss through cash, and others accept they can get genuine joy seeing someone. Some even feel that satisfaction must be gotten when dominating in their vocation.

As we would presumably know, joy is just the condition of being content and cheerful. Many individuals previously, present, and a few (even later on will) have attempted to characterize and clarify what they think satisfaction truly is. Up until this point, the most sensible one is the one that considers joy to be something that can just come from inside an individual and ought not to be looked for outside on the planet.

A great deal of us attempts to discover Bliss, where it isn't. We relate and compare cash with joy. If there is Bliss in cash, at that point, the entirety of the rich individuals we have around us could never feel miserable. What we have come to see is that even the rich among us are the ones that endure melancholy, relationship issues, stress, dread, and even uneasiness. Many big names and fruitful individuals have ended it all. This goes far to show that cash or notoriety doesn't ensure Bliss. This doesn't imply that it is terrible to be rich and follow the cash. When you have cash, you can manage the cost of numerous things that can make you and everyone around you upbeat.

There is an adage that clarifies that one can get genuine joy when one acknowledges that just one can make himself/herself cheerful. We can discover genuine joy inside ourselves and can't discover it in others. This expression and its significance are constantly pounded on in better places, yet we actually decline to get it completely and put it into great use. Significantly, we comprehend that Bliss is simply the condition of an individual's brain. Bliss can't emerge from the multitude of actual things we see around us. We can get past great considerations through our positive feelings and can make genuine joy.

Our considerations make our feelings. Subsequently, it is significant that we work on having just certain contemplations, which can be accomplished when we see life positively. Each individual wants Bliss. Nonetheless, not many people accomplish Bliss effectively throughout everyday life.

It isn't easy to get joy in life as individuals ordinarily connect it with the things and the individuals around them. The basic actuality is that Bliss typically begins just as it gets done with your own life. All of those individuals who comprehend this reality effectively get genuine satisfaction in their lives.

There are heaps of individuals who connect joy with cash, and there are not many others who interface it with individual relations. It is critical to realize that if you are not content with yourself, at that point, it is absurd to expect to stay glad in your relationship too.

The truth of the matter is that man has involved himself with the way to joy for centuries. During the advancement, something occurred that made us profoundly question the reason for our reality. Individuals like Buddha are essential for the appropriate response or attempt to offer us the answer. Since these inquiries have upset us, there have been numerous who tried to respond to them, and like this, they shaped methods of reasoning and religions. The quest for natural joy will cause numerous to carry out overwhelming things.But if this energy is utilized incorrectly, it can cause incredible anguish. How might we know which formula for satisfaction is the best one and what we ought to dedicate our time and consideration? We only have wrong statement here, so there is no correct answer, and as the introductory sentence of this article states, it is improbable to be cheerful because being glad is the way. That is how I got my head around this issue. Let me clarify some more.

To the detriment of sounding Buddhists, when you consider the majority of the things that make us miserable are material in nature. They are the things that we genuinely don't require, yet they cause us to feel happy. This thought isn't merely something the insightful man from the sixth century BC India communicated; however, many have said this when he, Socrates, and Jesus to give some examples.

I find intriguing the mystery present in the directions to arrive at it in the battle for Bliss. One has a belief all through life to be acceptable and persevering to get the things he continually needs later on in life, yet then as you begin to battle for the cash, you understand that your life is transforming into a cash getting game. In this way, the wellspring of joy and security turns into the abundance of all your tension and hostility. Naturally, we can perceive how a few people imagined that all material things remain on the way to our Bliss. In any case, shouldn't something be said about the unimportant, consider the possibility that you are enamored with somebody you shouldn't cherish? The above guidance would advise you to give up your profound longing, and you will be liberated from limitations. Is this Bliss? Or on the other hand, is it the battle to do and accomplish the unthinkable, the genuine wellspring of joy?

Individuals regularly fail to remember that they are creatures, and like every one of them, they have a rationale for their tendency and their particular requirements. Like the other whole creature's kin are trapped in the battle for the living. We now and again face challenges that can get you get trapped in some unacceptable conditions. Men have made themselves protected from a large portion of the things that might have hurt him in nature; however, in doing so, he failed to remember what he has made.

Consider the present from a historic viewpoint. The fact of the matter is we have a ton to appreciate in the current age, and the way that a few of us are troubled because we don't have our entire existence wants is only a manifestation of aggregate early stages. Having the entirety of your friends and family around you, with a rooftop to shield under and with bunches of delightful food, is the sole wellspring of joy man needs. All the other things should be a reward.

Joy can't be found by dismissing all that is material or bringing in more cash than you can spend. Try to discover balance by taking a gander at yourself and the lives of individuals around you. By understanding that there is a ton to be appreciative of, try to quit looking for a new income streams and comprehend that we are now strolling on one. However long we are making any rundown of the essential for our bliss life, we will wind up unsatisfied because life doesn't concede wishes. We are the ones that make them work out as expected. Regularly the most significant change in our lives comes from a fundamental difference in context instead of anything we can claim.

Our lives can be occupied with everyday exercises and obligations. A significant number of us perform multiple tasks, so we may race ahead, contemplating the next spot we should be in. However, easing back down to focus on the thing we're doing and why, it constructs Bliss.

Focus on the impacts of your activities. Notice the ways (large or little) that you affect. Carry on with life, dependent on the critical qualities to you. Set aside some effort to consider the main thing to you (like helping other people or ensuring the planet).

How would you like to make the world a prime spot? Notice any little everyday activities that point you toward that path. They help give your life a feeling of importance and increment joy.

Joy is a powerful feeling that impacts how we live and feel consistently. Joy is accomplished. Individuals have the freedom to pick pleasure since we are not limited by any conditions forever. Variables that impact satisfaction are those that add to enthusiastic prosperity. Real prosperity likewise influences joy. Each individual discovers Bliss on their own because they understand what makes them cheerful and what doesn't.

Satisfaction is an interior motivation. It is a definite feeling. Pride causes us to remain fit both intellectually and indeed. Joy helps in bringing down pressure and avoiding any medical problems. The explanation of satisfaction might be distinctive for various persons. It would be great that every one of us discovered what satisfies you. Along these lines, if you need genuine pleasure throughout everyday life, you need to comprehend that no one but you can fulfill yourself. The way to satisfaction lies in doing what one loves. Many individuals wind up having a contrite life, loaded up with laments; this happens because they settle for something that they don't genuinely like. Regardless of what the general public forces on us, we should enjoy just that which causes us to feel cheerful and happy.

One can't accomplish total and untainted satisfaction. Somebody can't stay in a condition of most extreme ecstasy and Happiness. We all have something reasonable of torments and laments throughout everyday life. Yet, there additionally are short moments of inconclusive and unlimited delights. We should all stick to those snapshots of Bliss and treasure them wholeheartedly to have a joyful life when it's all said and done. Although life tosses incalculable difficulties at us consistently, we would get discouraged on the off chance that we suffocate in those difficulties. Significantly, we discover good things in our day-by-day lives to get excited for and feel the Bliss.

Chapter 5:
Weight loss

If you take a look at Law of Attraction weight reduction examples of overcoming serious problems, one thing you'll find is that the individuals in these conditions have obvious motivation to get this done. This means that invest some energy recognizing your explanations behind getting more fit and investigating the convictions and suspicions.

To prevail with regards to utilizing the Law of Attraction for weight reduction, you need to plan uplifting objectives that cause you to feel better. Here, consider things like needing to have the endurance to ascend a mountain, take up another game, or pursue kids in your family. Regardless of whether you don't have specific positive exercises as a top priority, by and large, uplifting objectives can likewise work (for example, diminishing your chances of creating long-term medical conditions). So showing weight reduction is a lot simpler if you're ready to build up a cheerful, adoring disposition to your present body (not merely towards the body you envision creating later on). Positive speculation for weight reduction starts by upgrading your confidence and by being thankful for what you're ready to do at present.

In total, you'll need to discover at least one specific purpose behind shedding pounds; reasons that come from a position of confidence and a craving for development, not from self-hatred. If your reasons are negative, it will be a lot harder to accomplish your objective. This is because you'll be centered on thoughts regarding the need, disdain, and disappointment.

Taking such a step can be challenging, and it requires will and brainpower to go through all this=. Another significant part of your Law of attraction for weight reduction technique includes developing your intellectual competence. As you upgrade your psychological aptitudes, you improve your capacity to reason. It can likewise boost poise and give you extra energy.

A substantial weight reduction rate is essential to shedding pounds. Quick weight reduction through exceptional measures; for example, craze of consuming fewer calories, is short-lived, because these strategies are challenging to keep up long haul. The moderate digestion causes you to feel wiped out and drowsy, and the weight you lose, which is in all likelihood muscle and water weight, is immediately recaptured. A weight reduction pace of 1.5 pounds every week is sensible and falls inside the master's prescribed scope of 1 to 2 pounds. You can accomplish this by eating a solid, decreased calorie diet and performing ordinary exercise.

The body weight measure is utilized as an intermediary for the overabundance of muscle versus fat, and along with tallness, the weight list (BMI) can be determined. The BMI is defined as the weight in kilograms isolated by stature in meters squared (BMI = weight, kg/tallness, m2). The BMI is utilized to characterize the seriousness of excessive weight, which is fundamentally founded on the relationship between BMI and mortality. The BMI is dependent on sex and age.

Whenever you are going for weight loss, do the following:

• Eliminate any psychological hindrances to your prosperity and keep melancholic energy/musings away.

• Dress how you plan to when you shed pounds, make ways for the improvements

• And believe that your body is in perfect shape.

 • Transform behavior in ways that aid you to accomplish your weight loss goals

In the present quick moving climate, it is anything but difficult to embrace unfortunate practices. In the reason for obesity, analyze your food decisions, a measure of actual work you get, and the push to keep up your well-being. In light of food decisions, numerous individuals currently select weight control plans that are calorie-rich yet supplement poor. This social issue is also because of the expansion in eating out habits.

Environment assumes a vital part in forming a person's propensities and way of life. Numerous natural impacts can affect your well-being choices. The present society has built up a more inactive way of life. Walking has been supplanted by driving vehicles, actual essential work has been replaced by innovation, and sustenance has been overwhelmed by accommodation nourishments.

Feelings can likewise assume a part in overabundance weight. A few people manage pressure, uneasiness, or wretchedness by eating. This may help incidentally. However, it can likewise exacerbate the issue. "Passionate eating" can wind up hurting your psychological and actual well-being. That is why discovering approaches to adapt to sentiments and feelings can be a vital piece of any work to get in shape.

Hereditary qualities are also important in determining your tendency to determine weight. Science backs this point. Not all people inclined to plumpness will actually be obese. Further studies are being conducted to figure out which qualities contribute most to weight. In any case, getting thinner is regularly more confounded than only eating less and practicing more. Cutting calories and being more dynamic is essential; however, different sorts of changes might be expected to get thinner in long term. Luckily, numerous medical care suppliers can give you the direction and support that you need to get more fit and improve your well-being.

There are a few unique resources for getting thinner. A few people have medical surgeries, take pills, or starve themselves to arrive at this objective. The reason for this article is to look into the costs, medical advantages, and the results of weight reduction between these various techniques. The perfect way to get in shape is to eat well and exercise appropriately because this strategy is beneficial, and the outcomes are more specific.

During the most recent decade, innovation has gone so far that presently individuals get an unforeseen possibility of immediate difference in body and well-being. Weight reduction or medical procedure is a quick means of shedding pounds and getting a fit body. This kind of weight reduction isn't for everyone. It is suggested uniquely for those individuals who fizzle in some other technique for getting thinner or for the individuals who have genuine medical problems or extreme weight.

Another approach to lose or control weight is taking weight reduction drugs. They are endorsed for those who couldn't get thinner with some other strategy. Before purchasing any medicine, the individual ought to get help from a specialist on what sorts of medications are endorsed by the Food and Medication Organization (FDA) and have fewer sideeffects.

FDA endorsement shows that the medication is generally protected. There are two kinds of weight reduction pills: professionally prescribed medications and over-the-counter drugs. Physicians endorsed drugs, also called hostile to corpulence drugs, are recommended by the specialist in more extreme cases to those individuals who have genuine medical issues. They increment energy consumption, decline the quantity of retained calories, and stifle hunger. The results of this sort of drug are hypertension, expanded circulatory strain, heartbeat, and pulse, unsteadiness, sleep deprivation, clogging, retching. Over-the-counter or nonprescription medicine incorporates natural items or dietary enhancements. They are not difficult to purchase, and in contrast with doctor prescribed medications, they are less expensive. OTC eating routine pills contain spices that consume calories, smother craving, and abatement fat. The significant hindrance is that the FDA doesn't check it. OTC medications' primary symptoms are looseness of the bowels, liver and kidney harm, coronary failure, and even stroke. Remember that this kind of weight reduction isn't appropriate and may not work for everyone. Other than the preferred position of shedding pounds, all medications have a ton of results. Diet pills alone without standard active work and diet plan won't show any outcomes. The consultation with a specialist is compulsory before assuming any weight reduction prescription.

The best way is using mind power to cope with this weight loss power, be happy, and not let yourself down. Starvation is an outrageous food constraint to get more slender. Nevertheless, the outcome of hunger is the inverse. The nonappearance of calories keeps the supplements and minerals to be absorbed by the body, leading to weakness.

Fasting is an old practice, ordinarily used because of extreme viewpoints to learn patience. But if used for getting slimmer, it may have irreversible results. Today fasting accepts the use of water, juices, tea. Individuals quickly get in shape rapidly, yet they lose just body liquid, not fat. Fasting hinders a metabolic rate, so when the individual begins eating typical food once more, all the shed pounds will be recovered. Another kind of starvation is eating fewer carbs. Today we can discover countless such well known and individuals who eat fewer carbs, proposing to get in shape in a few days. Indeed, none of them will bring the ideal impact. Individuals counting calories are consistently unpleasant, discouraged, anxious, and angry. Any starvation prompts lopsidedness between energy taking and energy use. This awkwardness may cause dietary issues, for example, anorexia, an exceptional dread, or putting on weight that can prompt genuine medical conditions or bulimia, an illness when eating is trailed by intentional spewing. The indications of bulimia are like those of anorexia: losing a great deal of weight, declining to eat, being discouraged, and so forth.

There are multiple reasons of why an individual might need to shed pounds. Moderate decreases in weight might be accomplished by the fundamental way of life alterations.

In case your goal is prosperity improvement, recollect that eating fewer carbs may cause more harm than anything else. Weight decrease and weight gaining cycles can hurt the body. For example, the body doesn't merely lose fat when eating fewer carbs. Muscle misfortune happens to bring about what seems, to be perpetual lessening indigestion. Numerous other neurobiological components are battling against you to shield the body against weight reduction, including changes for chemicals and neuropeptides. This prompts trouble keeping up weight reduction. Prohibitive admission, otherwise known as counting calories, brings about food desires, which in the end lead to indulging, thus causing sensations of blame and disappointment. It resembles attempting to hold your breath – your body will dominate. Slimming down is additionally the main danger factor for building up a dietary problem. Exceptionally prohibitive eating regimens moderate digestion, causing it to consume energy and get more fit. The main concern: starvation prompts long term weight acquisition, regardless of whether you get more fit from the outset. Figuring out how to eat all food sources with some restraint and appreciate development is a positive way of life changes that will help you support your body and make the most of your involvement in food.

It might seem like skipping dinners is an approach to scale back calories and get more fit; however, this methodology ordinarily accomplishes more mischief than any good. Frequently, it prompts gorging and less reliable food decisions later in the day because you are eager. Likewise, not eating routinely (every 3 to 5 hours) may influence your focus, state of mind, and energy level.

All things being equal, eat carefully by tuning in to your body and figuring out how to distinguish and follow up on craving and prompts. Exploration shows that the individuals who eat carefully will, in general, settle on reliable decisions naturally and deal with their weight better throughout their lives. Eating carefully will help you distinguish the different reasons you eat, like pressure or negative feelings. Discover elective methods of managing these feelings like a hot cup of tea, hot shower, conversing with a companion, or going for a stroll.

The controlled sugar wholesome methodology isn't one of the bad ways to shed weight. Strong appetite is the principal purpose behind the disappointment of most weight reduction endeavors. A lifetime eating plan should be acceptable, charming, and filling. You should surrender sugar and other refined starches, for example, white flour. Yet, many people find that once they shake off the sugar dependence, they feel no powerful urge to return to it. For them, a healthful methodology that permits them to eat an immense assortment of meat and fish and plates of mixed greens and vegetables arranged in the most mouth-watering way, i.e., with spread and cream and flavors and spices, is not grim.

The issue with getting in shape on a low-calorie/low-fat eating routine or on a liquid protein diet is that the support program is different from the health improvement plan. So when you return to your previous eating method, the pounds get back at a fantastic rate since you are caught off guard for support. There are sound physiological purposes behind this. When the calories are limited, you eat, your digestion shifts into an endurance mode, which means it eases back down to preserve energy. At the point when you return to an unhealthier eating regimen as you unavoidably should, your body is still in its method of consuming calories gradually. So it turns out to be very difficult to proceed or keep up weight reduction.

The vast majority think about it that you can typically lose a ton of weight quickly. You most likely can. In any case, the main focus should be that the weight doesn't return. One reason is that it doesn't make a significant contrast in the number of calories you eat during the weight reduction and weight support stages.

When you are loaded with energy, you are more disposed to work out, improving weight reduction and supplanting fat tissue with muscle, which will likewise help you cut creeps from your estimations. Individuals will see the changes in you, upgrading your feeling of achievement and pride.

This arrangement is stable. More than once, research has exhibited that controlling starch admission brings about improved blood cholesterol and fatty substance levels, the balance of glucose levels, and a decrease of circulatory strain. Every one of these markers brings about the decreased danger for cardiovascular illness.

You need to be thin and incredible, you need to eat healthy meat and vegetable that individuals ate and remained healthy hundreds of years ago. You do not need to eat like a hare; you can eat like a person. You can appreciate fish, sheep, steak and lobster, nuts and berries, cheddar, eggs, and margarine alongside a magnificent assortment of a plate of mixed greens and different vegetables.

Keep the Law of attraction standards to help you shed pounds and keep a sound load forever. Here are a few hints that will assist you with accomplishing this assignment:

• Request the initial phase in utilizing the Law from Appreciation to make the existence you need.

Understand what weight you need to be, understand what size garments you need to wear, envision how you will feel when you have accomplished this.

• Accept: Envision how your life will be the point at which you have lost the weight.

Make a film in your psyche about how you will look and feel when eating a solid, adjusted eating routine and losing the weight you need to. What things will you have the option to do that you haven't had the opportunity to do? What new garments will you ready to purchase and wear? Who will you be the point at which you are sound and glad?

• Acknowledge that the human body was made for development.

Active work is essential to be trustworthy. Our joints were made for development, and if we don't utilize them, we will lose utilization of them. Their moderate measure of day-to- day exercise will shield you from sickness; it will consume additional calories to help in your weight reduction; and cause you to feel incredible because activity discharges serotonin, the excellent vibe chemical. At the point when you feel extraordinary, you are pulling in business as usual.

• Get: Make a positive move towards what you need and be available to accept.

Comprehend your body and understand what it needs

Explore sustenance to understand what a decent eating routine comprises of and why you need every segment. When you comprehend why you need proteins, new leafy foods, natural starch, and great fats, your mentality to them will improve. Have a positive outlook on your food and dinners, value your body and it attempts to support you. Be glad that you presently understand what you need to do to be sound and lose extra weight.

• Tune in to your own body.

Figure out how to tune in to your body and gives what it needs. Eat when you are eager instead of on specific occasions. Eat what your body discloses to you; it needs, not what society directs.

Keep in mind that you should not engage in any sensations of uncertainty, stress, or dread of disappointment. Disappointment isn't a chance with the Law of Attraction – keep just good emotions around your well-being, food, and weight.

Feel great that you, at last, have authority over your well-being and make a good move towards getting in shape. You will pull in a more significant amount of what you are feeling and keep getting more fit.

Decide to follow a controlled starch dietary methodology. It has nearly the same number of bundled and arranged food alternatives as individuals who seem to be, accidentally, following a low-fat eating routine. Visit your nearby food store, drug store, store, or even mass-market store, and you will see the wide assortment of food items accessible to somebody who comprehends the advantages of controlled sugar nourishment. Advances in the logical agreement have made you ready for options in contrast to food rich in starches, food sources, for example, pasta, bread, biscuits, cakes, sweets, and even frozen yogurt, also the wide assortment of energy bars and prepared to-drink shakes.

Regardless of whether you are experienced at the weight reduction game or have been on a detailed nutritional plan previously, the accompanying situation may sound generally very recognizable. Resolved to succeed, you promised to approach thinning down the "right" way. You quit eating red meat, cooked egg-white-just omelets with no oil in a Teflon container, eliminated the skin from chicken, ate your heated potato without margarine or sharp cream, and burned-through heaps of pasta: frozen yogurt, leafy foods filled in as a treat. Your morning meal comprises cereal and skims milk or, more likely, granola and a banana. A regular lunch was white-meat turkey on a roll and a liberal plate of mixed greens, without the dressing.

Even if you stayed with your low-fat routine and you realized it was the correct eating regimen because your loved ones praised you on your fit body. However, it never felt very ideal for you in some way or another. You found that you weren't satisfied out of your eating along these lines: You were frequently eager and low in energy, and to top it all off perpetual, critical weight reduction demonstrated an inadequate body mass reduction. You never really accomplished the objectives that persuaded you to start eating better in any case.

Set aside some effort to see and like the little changes in your body, your energy, your temperament, and the certainty you acquire from figuring out how to cherish and focus on yourself step-by-step. Do whatever it takes not to allow an apparent mishap to get you deterred from settling on better decisions. We're all individuals and shouldn't get everything right always. Additionally, don't contrast your eating routine with others that keeps you from eating carefully and frequently prompts disgrace, blame, and an entire wreck of other negative feelings that you don't possess energy for! Every individual is exceptional and has various requirements.

Interestingly, you can figure out how to change your way of life, lose much weight, and become better. You can gradually settle on better food decisions and incorporate more diligent work into your life. A Clinical Get-healthy plan or careful procedures might be possibilities for those with colossal overabundance weight.

Controlling excessive weight is a long-lasting struggle; however, you have made the principal strides on your excursion by perusing this guide. Work with your medical services supplier, and you will locate the best way towards progress and the numerous advantages of good weight.

Chapter 6:
Beauty

Beauty can be outer or inner or both. Outside or inner beauty is promptly obvious. In a perfect world, the two kinds of beauty are associated and spring from each other. The internal beauty anyway dwells inside the individual. It isn't evident or can't be seen. It is something that must be felt and detected. The character of an individual and an individual's idea anyway is named the internal beauty.

Principles of beauty have changed over time in light of changing social qualities. Generally, canvases show a wide scope of various principles for beauty. In any case, moderately youthful people with smooth skin, proportional bodies, and ordinary highlights have generally been considered the most excellent from the beginning of time.

Beauty, to me, is numerous things. However, I don't consider "actual beauty" that numerous individuals may consider when they hear that word. It is a lot more than that. To comprehend beauty's significance, we should initially characterize what beauty is. So, beauty is the sign of adoration in structure.

In the present society, changing one's appearance through hair tone, eye-to-eye connection, and having corrective medical procedures all appear to be the response to making the "enhanced you." So, is it conceivable to change the actual appearance by applying the Law of attraction for new great looks instead of dealing with our external appearances?

Nobody considers themselves monstrous. Those two things cannot exist together. Absolute beauty is both internal and external excellence. Inward beauty is the thing that individuals call mental self-view or confidence. If you trust you are ugly and terrible, regardless of what sort of garments or gems you wear or the amount you attempt to upgrade your appearance, you won't, in any case, ever be perfect. If we think and accept, we are not appealing, we will show individuals and conditions that fortify the conviction. We are conveying a recurrence to everyone around us that we are not extraordinary, and that will cover our actual excellence so individuals can't see it.

On the other hand, you trust you are lovely, paying little mind to your appearance, you will transmit excellence, which individuals will see. ow your magnificence is seen by society begins inside you. You can draw in others if you have an ideal Barbie doll figure. At the point when you can glimpse inside yourself and love your internal appearance, this certainty and satisfaction will emanate from your inward being, and that is the thing that others will be pulled into.

What your identity makes, the outcomes you get externally. When you change how you are inside, the external world changes, the energy you give out draws in and creates the results you get. Change your inward significance, and you change your outcomes.

Start inside and discover what you like about yourself. What are your blessings? Is it accurate to say that you are merciful to everyone around you? It is okay to say that you are thankful for what you have and glad yourself? Presently look in the mirror and see what you like from an external perspective. We as a whole tend to zero in on the things we are doing, like when we look in the mirror, and it is significant not to bring up the imperfections that you think you have. Rather center around the things you genuinely like about you, from within to the outside. Let those apparent "blemishes" fall away from plain sight and fill the forefront with what you want. Acknowledge each knock and mole and understand that these are a piece of you, yet they are not the inward you. When you start to see that you are much the same as every other person on this planet externally and that you are an extraordinary being regardless, you will begin to create an energy that becomes alluring to other people.

You will pull in the sort of individuals you need to be close to by adoring and tolerating your identity and expressing gratitude toward the Universe for the brilliant endowment of life it has offered you to make through. They will need to associate with you since you have something that numerous individuals don't have in beautiful looking pictures and other aspects of digital world. And that is a marvel from inside that is incredible to such an extent that your outward appearance becomes to others the view of what you feel about yourself. The inward you are the thing that has excellence.

To improve the Law of Attraction force, you can make excellent instructions. Confirmation is a sentence that is written in the present for with the expectation of replacing negative or restricting mindset. When you can change a conviction, the law of attraction can begin bringing you new stunning things. In a real sense, there are a large number of cycles you can use for your need for excellence and the law of attraction. Interestingly, here is a program that feels great and you even get results following 30 days of training.

From the outset, it may appear awkward. You probably won't accept what you are stating, "I am wonderful," which could be a gigantic hop at present. Or which could push old convictions to the surface, start by saying "I decided to start thinking", or "I aim to begin thinking".

Certifications for excellence will, in time, cause you to feel vastly improved towards how you look. In the long-term, you will begin to transmit inward magnificence, and how individuals see you and you see yourself will change. You can arrive at where all obstruction towards your appearance is delivered, and the law of attraction is allowed to show anything you desire.

There are numerous abstract types of beauty, yet none of those definitions arrive at the central reality of what excellence truly is and why it should matter to us.

We should adhere to something that exists as a well-known fact about beauty. Beauty and love go connected. Indeed, one conceives the other. Love conceives beauty, and genuine excellence moves love. The two together can make an upward winding of happiness and cognizance. The two things together can deliver a profound feeling of harmony - A feeling that everything is directly on the planet for us.

Genuine beauty is the impression of our creator. When we associate with that beauty, it motivates us and encourages us to feel better. Here is the thing that we learn. We discover that we are not attracted tofor offensiveness. We are repulsed by it. Then again, we appreciate beauty. We invite its essence into our lives!

This shows us something about our real essence, isn't that right? For the time being if we leave all the abstract meanings of beauty behind, we out of nowhere have astonishing lucidity about what our identity is. We can really see that we are part of the nature.

Why do we typically hate things like brutality, anguish, and grieving? This is because these things are not in concurrence with us. They talk about a condition where God isn't. They talk about a condition such that there is no life. Right when we experience such things, we understand that we are not in contact with God.

We are supreme magnets for magnificence in the entirety of its structures. We love it. We want it. It reconnects us with our maker. It helps us to remember what our identity is. We can get comfortable there and feel at peace. Evidently, we find a sense of contentment.

"Every beauty which is seen here below by persons of

perception resembles more than anything
else that celestial

source from which we all come ..."

— Michelangelo

Then again, we need to flee from the grotesqueness of dissension, outrage, dread, and the entirety of their appearances. We don't care for feeling isolated from our maker! We need to be at home in the chest of heavenly love consistently. There we discover all we might need or require. There we get ourselves. It is critical to develop brilliance in your life since it exists as your nearest actual association with God. It adjusts you to your real essence and that of your maker. It mitigates the spirit and fulfills you.

Genuine beauty brings such countless prizes. Internal excellence is the principal creation at that point that can show as external beauty in an exhibit of all its brilliance.

Consider your knowledge and expansion of the heavenly. When you are associated with your maker, you feel love. You feel harmony. You are satisfied. Since adoration transmits, it is normal for affection to communicate ostensibly. At the point when it communicates, it shows magnificence.

We quickly perceive genuine beauty since it elevates and energizes us. We realize naturally that this is an appearance of God.

Actual magnificence consistently starts with the made-up excellence first. Non-actual excellence can't be estimated, yet it can positively be felt. It radiates from the inside.

No physical beauty is seen showing through benevolence, love, gratefulness, agreement, delight, and harmony. These things prove that innovative, divine love is being developed and shown inside that person. When the internal beauty is felt, it will show up in the physical one. Possibly it is as basic as a grin. Or then again, perhaps it shows as a thoughtful gesture. Maybe it exhibits itself through some aesthetic creation. When we quit opposing our maker's consistently present love, we will normally look to communicate that affection by making excellence surrounding us in the actual world.

Developing excellence relies on a particular something. You're longing to be at one with your maker. It relies on you ,giving up obstruction and recognizing that you truly need the affection for your maker. You profoundly need that dedication, love, and presence of the heavenly. Stop justifying and putting ludicrous choices on yourself like you are a terrible individual or lacking something important.

Moreover, it helps if you understood that greatness has nothing to do with others' choices. Wonderfulness isn't something that can be judged. It should be felt—much equivalent to fondness. Remember, the two things go indivisibly. To start with, we should discuss your body. Disregard publicists' forms of excellence. That is counterfeit and has nothing to do with what we discuss here. The most genuine type of actual excellence has to do with well-being, dynamic quality, and inventive self-articulation. This all begins with confidence and self-acknowledgment. So deal with yourself, honor yourself, and don't hesitate to communicate with adoration.

Next is your external climate. ? You bend towards request over confusion? Why would that be? Since it reflects friendlines, which, mirrors the fundamental idea of creation, it encourages you to unwind and feel much improved. It encourages you to complete more and experience less pressure.

Much the same as you favor inward friendliness, you likewise normally lean towards external envvironment in your current circumstance. Both carry you closer to your maker.

Lastly, we should discuss being more mindful and inventive with your actual climate. You have an astonishing capacity to saturate your whole actual world with energy as a person. What sort of energy will that be?

Will it be the most noteworthy energy of adoration and motivation? Will it be the energy of your heart that treasures your actual feelings? Use cognizance and high-vibrational energy into your actual climate, and watch how everything changes.

The astonishing thing about this is that it doesn't make a difference if you're rich or poor. Indeed, even in the smallest of settings, you can make sparkling excellence in each thing you contact.

Start to investigate these thoughts in your own life, and you will begin to understand that God and your maker are exceptionally close within reach. You will begin to understand the astonishing force that you have when you open yourself to the reality of your eternality. A genuine indication of magnificence surrounding you will be the final product.

Will it be the most elevated energy of affection and motivation? Will it be the energy of your heart that esteems your actual climate? Put cognizance and high-vibrational energy into your actual climate, and watch how everything changes.

The astounding thing about this is that it doesn't make a difference if you're rich or poor. Indeed, even in the most pitiful settings, you can make shimmering excellence in each thing you contact.

Start to investigate these thoughts in your own life, and you will begin to understand that your God is extremely close nearby. You will begin to understand the astounding force that you have when you open yourself to the reality of your holiness. A genuine appearance of magnificence surrounding you will be the outcome.

Hence, we associate body and personality closely; we believe that social government significantly affects our idea of excellence, particularly in Asia, where industrialism and corporate greed are generally high.

Social development profoundly impacts Asian people inside the man-centric framework's relations. This is why women in these areas are often seen through the traditional lens of slimness to beauty.

Ladies are dependent upon what society characterizes as wonderful: little midsections, long legs, limited hips, long sparkling hair, white immaculate skin, and thin body. Men are decided by muscle, tone, shape, bushy or bald chests and whatever other manly attributes that decide magnificence today. Along these lines, it is observable that people's body size depicted in broad communications has consistently declined in size. This, as a result, speaks to the new excellence pattern in the public arena.

That being stated, people's self-perception is alluded to as sllim ideal media. The term 'meager ideal media' features that being slim is acceptable and attractive, regardless of whether it harms one's well-being. Thus, dietary issues are frequently identified with ideal body generalization disguise. Scientists later found that anorexic and bulimia result from that drive to be thin, resulting from being disappointed with one's looks.

As per well-being scientists Schwartz and Brownell, the connection between weight and self-perception are perplexing. They contend that self-perception may be influenced by obesity through mental trouble, affecting life quality.

Gorging is normal among individuals with dietary problems and individuals who are obese. The investigation uncovers that gorging that isn't trailed by cleansing may influence weight to acquire. From a mental perspective, obesity is perhaps the most deriding wonders. Hence, being fixated on the slim ideal idea of magnificence or excellence in bends can be significant, as both are at huge well-being dangers. Through this, helpful guidelines get an opportunity of being re-imagined.

True excellence is the condition of being valid and true in a manner that stretches out affection to yourself and other people. It feels genuine, protected, alive, lively, streaming, credible, nurturing. This reality doesn't imply that excellence has anything to do with our garments or hair or bodies or faces.

Chapter 7:
Healing

In all honesty, the law of attraction is ground-breaking at assisting individuals with better well-being, generally speaking. Whether you need to get thinner or deal with your weight better, feel less focused, diminish the measures of a throbbing pain, you think. Or experience better recuperation times from diseases and wounds, or rest better and experience more superior energy levels, the law of attraction can help.

The law of attraction is instrumental with well-being since it highlights numerous exercises known to help lower anxiety feelings. Bringing down stress has been connected to a diminished danger of sickness and injury and improved well-being levels in general. No matter what situation you are facing; having low esteem and thoughts to succeed, ;either spiritual healing or physical healing in both ways law of attraction helps. In spiritual, it uplifts and shows you the perfect way and be aware they are many things around us that need to be inspired as well. So far, for physical, it encourages to heal either way you want. Regardless of whether you need to improve muscle tone, increase strength, rest better, oversee infections better, or in any case, experience - more noteworthy well-being brought down feelings of anxiety - can significantly help. The law of attraction can help you zero in your body on mending and carrying on with a stable life in general.

Achievement in this world is consistently a matter of individual exertion. However, you may be deluding yourself if you accept that you can prevail without others' co-activity. Achievement involves the most extraordinary effort just to the degree that each individual should choose what is needed as far as they could tell. This includes the utilization of a "creative mind." Starting here on, making progress involves ably and thoughtfully actuating others to co-work.

Before you can ensure co-activity from others, nay before you reserve the privilege to request or anticipate co-activity from others, you should initially show an ability to co-work with them.

One thing that is generally communicated in the law of attraction is this: if you determinedly keep your consideration and spotlight on negative and unfortunate musings, you will encounter actual signs of that through sickness. Keep in mind that the logical side of this is the pressure that these contemplations welcome. At the point when you center reliably around considerations, for example, "I'm continually going to be overweight, I can't get my eating leveled out," at that point, you surrender your control to food. You basically assert that within sight, you can't shield yourself from eating undesirable decisions or indulging within view of food. For musings, for example, "I won't ever carry on with a glad life due to my constant disease or my life failures," you unknowingly insist that your disease or your problem will consistently be in charge of your life and that you won't ever have the option to be cheerful accordingly. Most of the contemplations you believe are surrendering your capacity to sickness or your failures, basically removing your ability to have a sound and pleasant life despite these things. The law of attraction works best on your physical, mental, and passionate well-being at the point when you set aside and think about it thoroughly. This implies that you can't anticipate that it should change for the time being. Almost certainly, the considerations you have been having encompassing your well-being and health have existed for quite a while. Indeed, as indicated by geneticists, they may not have a place with you. The musings you have about your well-being might be acquired through your hereditary cosmetics. They may likewise be instructed to you through your social molding growing up. For example, if you had a nearby relative who much of the time communicated that they were in reliable weakness and outside their ability to control to take care of it.

The explanation you are in weakness now, regardless of whether it is transitory or persistent, is likely made through musings that you may not know about. As of now, been rehearsing mindfulness, you may not understand that you are reliably thinking musings that are keeping you from effectively moving past your infection and chronic sickness.

The law of attraction to improve your well-being and health is a progression of customs that you can rehearse consistently. These customs will help you make a space where you can quickly rehearse the law of attraction and welcome the advantages of your activities. We will zero in on how these customs fit into the six-venture cycle of showing that I plot already, beginning at this point. Request what you need. Concerning requesting great well-being, it is straightforward! State what you need, obviously and sympathetic.

With this lovely gift, our higher force has given us, we can fix any physical and mental infection. We can fix fears and weight issues. We can resolve any turmoil we have. If you are brought into the world with a disorder or sickness, you will most likely be unable to fix it. Yet, you will have the option to live an ordinary and better, more satisfying life by utilizing the LOA, even with these issues. We have an obscure thought of what we need; however, ambiguity isn't sufficient for the Universe to precisely see what we need. Utilizing a rundown and perusing it every day helps insert these fantasies of our own into our psyche minds – into our memory, which is how to get what we need. When we have precisely what we need to be remembered, it guarantees that we can request something very similar each time we imagine. If the points of interest of what we are asking are somewhat unique about what we asked for the last time, this prompts disarray concerning what The Universe thinks you need. When the Universe is confounded concerning what you need and what it trusts you as of now have (or don't have), it is incomprehensible for IT to offer it to you.

"Self-realization means that we have been consciously

connected with our source of being. Once we have made this

connection, then nothing can go wrong...."

— Swami Paramananda

When you compose your list of what you need to accomplish throughout everyday life, your well-being desires should go on that rundown. Suppose you have an ailment or sickness that you are trying to fix or change, at that point, record this on your list of objectives. And suppose you end up with a problem after you have just composed your rundown; at that point, update the rundown. Your wishes for well-being can be as necessary or as convoluted as you wish.

A large number of the more genuine illnesses are consistently likely to fix also. Indeed, even AIDS has been archived being restored by utilizing The LOA. Notwithstanding, remember the conversation about how your psyche should wholeheartedly accept that what you are requesting will happen in your life. unfortunately, this is a lot harder to do with your more genuine sicknesses. Explore different avenues regarding what your brain is prepared to do while simultaneously searching out the clinical consideration you need.

Life is testing. The future is unknown. Everything exists in a person. Everything lays on the idea. They are the building squares of life. The entire world, country, or society can be changed with merely a thought or an idea. The law says that what one thinks one turns into that'. The psyche gets blurred by such countless musings. If the brain can't distinguish a negative idea, it might detain one, and it might administer one's life. Whatever lies in the inward world is reflected outside? The decision to become glad or miserable exists in oneself. Great masterminds of the world never get overpowered by melancholic musings of uneasiness, outrage, discouragement, or stress. They include control inside oneself. First, it is necessary to mend the interior world that is the mind, distinguish a negative image that creates a sensation of contention in the mind. So, it gets most essential to adjust contemplations appropriately. If one feels appreciative and love for whatever conditions or situation one will be entrapped in, one can pull in great results and experience joy inside. Money, position, achievement, and connections are only a boost in reacting to positive considerations. Satisfaction is an emotional solace that is to feel calm inside oneself. To make bliss, to have an upbeat existence is only a decision to make with the right idea.

If you are wiped out, read your list of objectives every day, even a few times each day. Consistently tell you are more powerful how glad and grateful for the well-being that you do have and afterward be thankful that your significant illnesses are as of now on their approach to being mended. It would help if you lived as you have never had the affliction in any case. Clinical consideration combined with utilizing your intellectually inspirational disposition will carry more well-being and accomplishment to you than looking for clinical review alone.

Use parody, companions, and fun occasions to keep your spirits up as frequently as you can. You need to smile and snicker as much as possible.

Intervening is acceptable to use to help mend your body. Locate a tranquil place and spend a couple of moments daily doing this activity, close your eyes and unwind. At that point, start from the highest point of your head. Envision a

white light or any vision that indicates positive energy and well-being. White usually is fantastic. This tone is an indication of well-being. Envision this whirl around your head and pull out any pessimism. At that point, the vortex will proceed around your chest and stomach territory. Whenever you have completed this cycle, you can make it one stride further if you'd like and envision this virtue whirling through the internal parts of your body. Feel it go around the entirety of your real organs, muscles, and ligaments, and so forth; you can even envision this supernatural twirl going through your circulation system and veins. At that point, watch it as it blasts, sending each negative idea, sickness, affliction, agony, infection, or debasement out as distant from your body as conceivable. So goes the negative thoughts.

Feeling excellent and glad forestalls infection and affliction. When you become ill, it isn't simply because you have gotten it from somebody, yet it likewise because your feelings were not beneficial. Illness and ailment can't live in a sincerely healthy body. It is conceivable to fix yourself by having a positive point of view. Notwithstanding, it is a lot simpler to forestall ailment in any case by having an inspirational mentality than it is to fix it. Keeping yourself genuinely glad, grateful for each easily overlooked detail you have, appreciative for your abilities, thankful for the air and the existence that you have been given will assist with guaranteeing that you live bounteously in all parts of your life; cash, well-being, love, companions, and force would all be able to be yours.

Contemplating and envisioning your dream body is an extraordinary method to help you genuinely anchor in what you need and stay zeroed in on accomplishing it. The accompanying contemplation will help you get what you need your body to resemble, and how having this body will transform you. When you are ready, plunk down in a pleasant situation and guarantee that you are in a spot where you want to be. By then, start going with reflection.

Your muscles are conditioned, you are trustworthy, and you look astonishing. The entirety of your wellness objectives have materialized, and you can see yourself glancing back at you. The reflection is alluring to such an extent that you nearly can't accept it. However, you realize that this is you gazing back at yourself. You run your biceps and abs and set aside the effort to feel what they feel like, seeing how they are genuine and not merely a hallucination of your psyche. You notice how imperative and new you look and how energetic your new constitution makes you show up. You fit into the garments you have wanted to find a way into for such a long time, looking alluring and rounding them out entirely in the entirety of the correct spots. You grin and look past your appearance to perceive what is out of sight. Unexpectedly, you see things in the foundation that make you smile. In the foundation of the individual in the mirror, everything that speaks to your new, fit life is available. You see, a kitchen loaded up with healthy food, indications of running shoes, exercise garments, furthermore, other wellness gear in the front. Your place looks spotless and new, intently taking after how you feel as of now in your life. It looks so comfortable and natural like that spot is yours.

Furthermore, that is because it is yours. That is your life, as you have longed for it and as you need it. Without speculation, you venture into the mirror. Somewhat frightened, you peer down at yourself and notice that you are currently the body you were taking a gander at. Your abs are conditioned, your muscles are reliable, and you look and feel extraordinary. You turn upward and investigate the room around you, seeing how lively your life is since you are truly fit. Take in your new life for a couple of seconds, presently, as you unwind and appreciate what it seems like to have accomplished the entirety of your wellness objectives. At the point when you are prepared, you can open your eyes.

The law of attraction is superb for drawing in the life you want. Regardless of whether you need to pull in another way of life, upgrade your current way of life, or add things to your life that are not right now present, you can easily approach the law of attraction in start bringing in the entirety of the encounters and advancements that you want. The law of attraction is a magnificent and adaptable instrument that can be used to plan the existence you wish to and co-make it close by the widespread ground-breaking powers. The law of attraction doesn't know limits, and it isn't confined to just a little or evident appeal. You can pull in any wild or extraordinary encounters you can invoke in your psyche. Suppose you have wanted experience, yearning for a more beneficial or pleasant way of life, or need to have a truly incredible experience. In that case, the law of attraction can help you accomplish that. In this part, you will find out about how you can authorize the regulation of appreciation for your life with the goal that you can start driving the existence you want quickly. Before we get into showing and pulling in mind-boggling experiences like gathering celebrated individuals or finishing the most out of control encounters on your list, or turning out to be acclaimed yourself, we are going to zero in on how you can start executing the law of attraction on your everyday life to encounter a sponsor generally. At that point, you will begin learning how you can implement this superb law to improve your life specifically. Before we start investigating straightforward ways to improve your life, we should examine how you can utilize the law of appreciation to help you start living a more pleasant and exciting life every day in new and astounding manners. While you can unquestionably draw in and show explicit encounters, similar to what you will learn about later in this part, you can likewise free yourself up to draw in and get brilliant meetings out of the blue. If you need to wind up being showered with great and surprising encounters, start making these changes in your everyday life.

Request to get a magnificent life loaded up with shocks and beautiful encounters. Every morning when you rise, ask the Universe how you can be honored with brilliant, unforeseen meetings that will fill your heart with joy, euphoria, and significance. At the point when you are asking, don't request anything explicit. All things being equal, state your inquiry in a manner, for example, "How might I have a magnificently unforeseen surprise and how can my day be pleasant today?"

Accept that you, as well, are deserving of accomplishing brilliant things. You might be watching and filling your online media and existence with extraordinary records of individuals who have gotten great surprises in their everyday lives. For a few individuals, it is by all accounts a typical event. Each time you pivot, they appear to commend another for the astonishing experience that has happened with them. Accept that you, as well, are deserving of these brilliant encounters and that you can appreciate them in your own life! Accept that total sudden circumstances are falling into your lap on an interminable premise, with boundless potential for what they might be. There isn't anything distinctive among you and those who get infinite sudden gifts on a simple premise, beside convictions. Tune into a similar conviction framework, and you will start seeing great surprises in your way, as well! Envision a day-to-day existence where everything occurs for you. It is pronounced that everything happens for an explanation and that things are happening for you every day. Set aside the effort to accept that life is occurring for you by envisioning this. Picture not just the kinds of great things that could happen for you yet also how you will respond to sudden conditions. Will you get baffled and upset about changes in your way and surprising circumstances that emerge, accordingly driving them away? Or will you invite them with great affection; grasp all that they have to bring to the table you? No one but you can respond to this. Envision yourself doing the last mentioned, envision the entirety of the astonishing and energizing new encounters that fall into your lap because you are willing to get and acknowledge changes agenuinely.

Act no uniquely, in contrast, to you ordinarily do, more often than not. Generally, practically approach your day! Surprising gifts are only that: unforeseen. While you ought to expect that they will occur for you, don't go about like you are just sitting tight for them. Continue ahead like a normal day. The activities you might need to change are how you get your endowments and unforeseen circumstances. Be happy to adjust to change and grasp things that fall into your way. Try not to get effortlessly vexed and disappointed when things don't go as planned, as this will tell the Universe that you don't need these incredible gifts. This will conflict with the law of attraction and bring about you not getting what you have requested.

Your unforeseen gift might be little, for example, discovering five dollars or getting an espresso when you are grinding away, or it might be huge, for example, meeting somebody renowned or being skilled in a vehicle or a house. Get your approval transparently, regardless of how little or enormous it could be. Search for things that you got every day and become used to accepting them. An extraordinary way to do this is to record them and offer thanks each time you do.

Julia Meadows

Feedback

In a society we live in, which is culturally fixated on estimating ability and capacity, we regularly disregard the significant job of Law of attraction and motivation. The Law of attraction stirs us to additional opportunities by permitting us to rise above our everyday encounters and restrictions. It pushes an individual from indifference to plausibility and changes how we see our own capacities. Also, it may sometimes be disregarded due to its subtle nature. The association of experiences generated by law of attraction as heavily hasn't helped the individuals. Yet, as latest research shows, the Law of attraction can be enacted, caught, and controlled, and it majorly affects significant life results. As compared with the typical encounters of regular day-to-day existence, the Law of attraction includes raised degrees of positive affect and lower harmful affect levels.

And it isn't a one-time stimulus to generate a particular effect,.. Contrasted with being in an energetic and energized state, individuals who enter an enlivened state (by thinking about an earlier second the Law of attraction inspired them) detailed more prominent degrees of heavenliness and importance. Though specific influence is enacted when somebody is gaining ground toward their nearby, cognizant objectives, the Law of attraction is more identified with an enlivening to something new, better, or more significant: excellent quality of one's past concerns.

You can transform yourself in any capacity you trust you can. You are the same as any other individual, as they are the same as you. We are, for the most part, fit for outright achievement. It's just the ones who know this and accept with their entire being that they can make their significance. It is only the individuals who trust themselves to get their importance. It is as if the individuals expect nothing to make their existence of pure energy. There are no impossible dreams. Remember that the incomprehensible something that may appear from the start isn't just a chance, however precisely the thing you ought to focus on. Reach upwards; anticipate high.

You are a fantastic thing in this world destined to do and become anything you wish. It would be best if you initially sorted out what you actually need. Second, you should make a healthy pledge to yourself that nothing will hinder you. Third, you should have total confidence that you are more noteworthy than you ever realized you were and more equipped for anything that you ever thought previously. You should request all that you need in life to find a way to get you there.

As you have learned in this book, it isn't as necessary as asking, accepting, and getting. There is substantially more to it. In any case, when you venture out of your ideal street, there is just a single approach. Keep going toward that path you so want. Become the individual you need to be. Need it with all your being. Request it. Accept that you will have it. At that point, let it go-let The Universe have total.

Control without waiting for when and how, and I guarantee, you will be offered all the responses and instruments you will require to get you to your cravings. Be grateful for all that you as of now have, and don't worry over the things you don't have. Adore and appreciate everybody without enviously. The more you adore and appreciate others, the more others will cherish and respect you.

So, it should not be said when things turn out badly in your life and issues heap up, consistently, returning your intuition to the negative. Then what?

If you notice that you appear to draw in issues out of nowhere, make yourself mindful that you are not caring for your musings. Old convictions may have begun to crawl once again into your considerations. You might be found pondering what isn't going right. This response is typical when a progression of calamities hits us; the more we stress over things turning out badly, the more things turn out badly. It is an endless loop!

That is actually what you need to do! Quit going around extinguishing the wildfires and take time to plunk down and zero in on where you are, what you need to accomplish, and afterward go after the best feeling you can discover. Do this through appreciation; learn something that is functioning admirably and be thankful for it. Zero in on this accomplishment until you begin to feel much improved. Slowly search for different functioning things admirably and be grateful for them to raise your vibration significantly.

A helpful procedure on occasions, such as this, is to advise yourself that what you are encountering is an impermanent mishap. Purposely center around something beneficial and offer thanks for the positive qualities in your life. This will help you switch things around back in support of yourself. Quite a bit of what we have pulled in our lives isn't finished by intentional aim, in any case, comes to an end, as a matter of course, because of our opinion about it. Persistent musings about undesirable things welcome, and pull in, coordinating encounters.

Keeping an uplifting mentality is an effective and significant practice to arrange the preparation for working with the Law of Attraction. Since our contemplations' entirety creates our encounters, remaining mindful of when your considerations go negative, and returning them on an upbeat track will assist in populating your future meetings with positive ones.

Coincidentally, don't permit yourself to pummel yourself if you incline to go negative throughout everyday life. That adds another layer of self-judgment that does you nothing but evil. Do all that can be expected to remain positive and read on for additional experiences and practices to help you turn that around. As a solitary strategy to draw in explicit encounters, individuals, accomplishments, and things that we want in our lives, thinking emphatically misses the mark. We'll investigate what else is essential to drive your longings to turn into your new experience truly.

When you know precisely what it is you need, take this expression and make it as explicit as conceivable to what you need to accomplish. You can abbreviate this in any capacity that you like so long as you keep the parts that you find generally critical to you. Likewise, recollect that you don't have to have gotten these things done as of now. You are preparing your brain psychology to accept that they have as of now occurred, so your substantial activities will take action accordingly.

This expression might be hard to accept. Express this principal couple of times to yourself. In any case, the more extended and all the more regularly you remain exposed to this expression, the more you will begin to trust it. You will start to grin. You will begin to feel excited about it. When that confusion shows up, express the same feeling a couple of more times and you'll see the difference.

You might want to know how can this be done? You may begin standing before the mirror and saying it to you for a long time. Aftre leaving the mirror you will right about the thing you are disclosing to yourself. In case you start questioning your activity, you'll be conveying negative energy about it into The Universe.

I do this consistently. I have my negative suspicious minutes, and however, at the point when I do this, it lifts my spirits. Indeed, even for the duration of the day while I'm cleaning my house or shopping for food, I will make statements like this to myself. I don't know whether it's something that I will one day not have to do any longer or if it's something that, indeed, even the individuals reading this actually need to do from time-to-time. I realize that it works and that I will do it as many times as required. This ought to be done whenever you notice your feelings slipping into a hostile region. You can utilize this for each part of your life.

I rehash something very similar over until I feel upbeat about it. At that point, I let it go. Ensure that each time you utilize positive self-talk, which ought to be very frequently, you express gratitude toward The Universe every single time. I don't merely mention to myself what an extraordinary person I am. Yet, I additionally thank my maker for what an incredible guy I am, and for bringing me my excellent family in any case. Now and again, it is difficult for us to get ourselves in our melancholic musings. That is the thing that our emotions are there for. Clearly, when we feel awful, those sentiments are being brought about by our negative contemplations. When you notice that you are feeling terrible or feeling down, attempt and sort out what you are thinking that is causing these feelings in you. Utilize this to get yourself and turn your considerations around. When your concerns are non-convoluted, it makes it simpler to turn your emotions around as well. This is likewise critical to accomplish for your actual wellbeing as well.

Conclusion

The Law of attraction is the energy around us that should be upheld to help accomplish what we most desire on the planet. The body is a driving concentration with the energy in the Universe , to get everything that is wanted without exception, to the capacity to make a huge difference in our current world. But this is the Law that stops the vast majority as far as they can tell with the Law of attraction; they don't see how things work.

When allowing the law of attraction to play its role, a vibration is made with the Universe, with what is being wanted most; subsequently, that is the thing that is being pulled in to you, and that is the Law of attraction.

Individuals have restricted convictions about what they can or can't have. Frequently individuals become involved with their regular daily existences of living without change. In this way molding our conviction framework to imagine that we do not influence what changes we make in our lives. We keep on making the story that we have encountered in our lives, not triumphing; this story plays more than once. The narrative of I don't deserve what I'm requesting, or my restricted conviction of what has occurred in the past will happen once more. This narrative impacts our entire life and this is what we start seeing in our lives too. Self-esteem is a significant region of not getting what you need. Individuals center around an absence of achievement from an earlier time and adhere to those examples and conditions. The interference of the restricted story and conviction breaks individuals out of that old example. A lot of our longing to be effective is dependent on the decision and breaking of those old examples of repeating a similar activity repeatedly. The Law of Attraction states we create things, events, circumstances, and people who come into our lives are because of our thoughts and feelings. This means that we can have, do, or become anything that we choose by using our thoughts positively.

On the flip side, because there is no way around this universal Law, the reverse is also true. We create every one of our own negative circumstances simply by the thoughts and emotions we send out into The Universe.

The Universe loves and adores you and provides you with what you ask for daily. If what is showing up in your life is not what you desire, you need to look at your life from the Inside Out.

Everything starts within. As you only have the power of YOU to view this world with (at this moment), a clean the lens. Maybe it's time to let go of those things that no longer serve you. Maybe it's time to revisit your belief structures, release and forgive those people who have caused you pain learn to love yourself deeply and completely find things that make you happy in life, and pursue these with vigor (no stalking allowed), maybe you to need to slow down and have a long look at your life. The Universal Laws are the essential standards of life; they can't be transformed; they can't be broken, and they exist if you trust in them. The same laws apply to each individual at each edge of the globe.

There isn't anything more significant than ensuring you feel better. From the passionate condition of feeling better, you can make the existence you need.

See what you need, comprehend what it will intend to have it, have a positive outlook on it, and you will pull in business as usual.

Continue to go after an imagination that feels improved. Your feelings are your manual for lining up with the vibrations of what you need. Having faith in The Law of Attraction is something magnificent. There is no limitation of using it in your favor. For some, accepting isn't an issue, but it's constantly keeping their feelings at a high and cheerful recurrence, which becomes a problem.

We, as a whole, have our awful minutes. Indeed, even individuals who have been considering and utilizing The Law of Attraction have negative contemplations for quite a long time.

We can't forestall them totally, and as said previously, we truly don't have any desire to, for they come from our cognizant brain, which is something we need for our own security. While this method of seeing the world may be hard to process for some. When you comprehend our interest in negative, things become much more straightforward. We are all searching for alleviation from the struggle. In the event that we don't really accept that we can resolve the contention remotely, we habitually make a way to settle itself inside. This is frequently found in games. At the point when a competitor isn't performing admirably or has an off the field strife, he regularly endures a physical issue. While the injury may be genuine (a pulled hamstring or a solid back), the psyche was hectically grinding away, making the circumstance. Fans would substantially more likely uphold a player if he was harmed than having conjugal issue at home.

A competitor is required to leave his private matters off the field or court. You don't need to put stock in the Law of Attraction for it to be working. Just as you don't need to comprehend or know about gravity, it is as yet working. Step off an overhang of a two-story building, and if you trust in gravity, you will probably still come colliding with the ground. The vast majority make as a matter of course, implying that they don't know about what their musings are and thus assume no liability when their indications show up—to improve things or make them more awful.

In the event that you don't figure out how to play the game, it will unquestionably play you. We are discussing the psyche game going on within you. At the point when you are an oblivious attractor of your world, you frequently become a casualty and are stuck at fault. This is the point at which the game is playing you. A brain in a condition of thankfulness is a psyche making positive outcomes. A brain searching for a person or thing to fault is a brain making more harm and mayhem in one's life. If you put reliance in the Law of Attraction, it doesn't make a difference. The brain's force is still in place, and the outcomes can be felt at present. Wouldn't you say it good to figure out how to center your considerations and begin to get the entirety of the fantasies that have you been requesting?

References

- Napoleon Hill, Think and Grow Rich: The Andrew Carnegie, Random House, 1960.

- Hicks, E. .T. (2006). The law ofattraction. Carlsbad, CA: Hay House

- Merer, .T. (2008). Attracting anything. San Diego, CA: Universe Press

- Harris, P. (2007). The early roots ofthe law ofattraction. St. Albert, Alberta: Avatar, 2007 Kathode Ray Enterprises, LLC Bargh, Raymond, Pryor, & Strack, 1995

- Chen, Lee–Chai & Bargh, 2001). (Guinote, Judd, & Brauer, 2002

- Anderson & Berdhal, 2002; Berdahl & Martorana, 2006

- (cf. Keltner et al., 2003), (Watson & Clark, 1997).

- (Hecht, Inderbirtzen, & Bukowski, 1998; Kupersmidt & Patterson, 1991; La Freniere & Stroufe, 1985).

- (Fiske, 1993; Keltner et al., 2003).

- (Goodwin, Gubin, Fiske, & Yzerbyt, 2000). Robbins, A. (1989). Unlimited power. New York,

- Dr. David R. Hawkins, Power Versus Force, Veritas Publishing, 1995, p. 263.

- Neill, M (2008). Feel happy how. Carlsbad, CA: Hay House
- Dyer, Wayne. Inspiration: Your Ultimate Calling. Hay House, 2006.
- Carnegie, Dale. How to Win Friends & Influence People. Pocket Books, 1936.
- Imagination to Create What You Want in Your Life, Nataraj Publishing, 2002.
- Hawkins, Dr. David R. I, Reality and Subjectivity. Veritas Publishing, 2002.
- Hicks, E. .T. (2006). The law ofattraction. Carlsbad, CA: Hay House
- Harris, P. (2007). The early roots ofthe law ofattraction. St. Albert, Alberta: Avatar
- Hay, Louise L. and friends, Gratitude A Way of life. Auustralia: Hay House India, 2013.

Printed in Great Britain
by Amazon

15598343R00079